Self-Interest and Social Order in Classical Liberalism

Self-Interest and Social Order in Classical Liberalism

THE ESSAYS OF
GEORGE H. SMITH

CATO INSTITUTE
WASHINGTON, D.C.

eBook ISBN: 978-1-944424-40-4
Print ISBN: 978-1-944424-39-8

Library of Congress Cataloging-in-Publication Data available.

Printed in the United States of America.

CATO INSTITUTE
1000 Massachusetts Avenue, N.W.
Washington, D.C. 20001
www.cato.org

CONTENTS

1. Political Philosophy and Justice 1

2. David Hume 13

3. David Hume on Justice 25

4. Thomas Hobbes 37

5. The Selfish System 51

6. Joseph Butler 61

7. Joseph Butler, Continued 71

8. Bernard Mandeville 81

9. Mandeville on the Benefits of Vice 93

10. Bernard Mandeville vs. Francis Hutcheson. 103

Notes 113

Index 115

Political Philosophy and Justice

Political philosophy is a systematic inquiry into the nature of a good society and its preconditions, implications, and corollaries. The political philosopher, in framing his conception of a good society, must engage in two kinds of investigation: *normative* (or prescriptive) and *positive* (or descriptive). The normative part of political philosophy is concerned with the nature of *justice*, whereas the positive part is concerned with the nature of *social order. What is justice? What is social order?* These fundamental questions, when considered in tandem, establish the field of inquiry for that discipline known as political philosophy. (Another descriptive feature of political philosophy is its theory of human nature, which is the ultimate foundation for everything else. I discuss this issue in later chapters.)

We sometimes think of political philosophy as essentially prescriptive while neglecting its descriptive features. This is an understandable oversight, for justice has traditionally been regarded as the core concept of this discipline. But no theory of justice can be (or ever has been) defended without a corresponding theory of social order. This latter may be tacitly assumed or implicitly contained within a theory of justice, but it is there nonetheless. A philosopher may be unaware of these descriptive elements, he may not have clearly formulated his theory of social order or worked out its implications, but he cannot avoid the fact that *justice is a social concept.* A theory of justice expresses an ideal relationship—that is, a relationship that *ought* to exist—between two or more individuals. We can act unjustly only toward others, never toward ourselves.

Plato?
Smith?

Thus, in formulating a theory of justice, the philosopher must consider what would probably happen if his moral ideal were accepted and acted upon in the real world. Would his ideal of justice promote cooperation or conflict, harmony or chaos, abundance or poverty, happiness or misery? No philosopher, of course, will endorse the negative side of these dichotomies. No philosopher will claim that his theory of justice, if implemented, would result in perpetual conflict,

2

Two kinds — necessary vs sufficient conditions for good society

chaos, poverty, or misery. We may therefore ask the philosopher how he knows all this. On what basis does he presume that his theory of justice is at least consistent with a minimal degree of social order—that it would not, for example, plunge society into that Hobbesian nightmare, that state of perpetual war of every man against every man where life is "nasty, brutish, and short"?

It is when answering such questions that the political philosopher must rely upon a theory of social order. And this is where the philosopher must venture beyond his native domain of ethics into the foreign territories of sociology, economics, social psychology, and other human sciences.

Political philosophies may be divided into two broad categories, or ideal types. The first assigns to political theory the limited task of determining those general conditions that are *necessary* for a good society. The second assigns to political theory the more expansive task of determining, not only those conditions that are necessary for a good society, but those that are *sufficient* as well.

By "necessary," I mean those conditions without which a good society cannot exist. Such conditions are essential but minimal; they establish general principles of justice and social order without prescribing in detail how these principles should be implemented in particular cases. Political philosophy, thus

3

conceived, can lay down general rules while leaving considerable room for social and cultural variations, the specifics of which will often depend on historical circumstances that are unique to a given society.

By "sufficient," I mean those conditions that will result in the best of all possible societies. In contrast to a theory of necessary conditions, which specifies the preconditions of a good society, a theory of sufficient conditions attempts to draft a social blueprint, in effect, often in considerable detail. Or, to use more familiar terms, a theory of sufficient conditions is a theory of social planning.

A theory of necessary conditions will tend to generate a model of the open society, whereas a theory of necessary *and* sufficient conditions will tend to generate a model of the closed society. These conflicting models result from the inner logic of ideas. To offer a sketch of what is minimally necessary for a good society is to leave considerable room for diversity, variation, and change. But the available space for individuality will progressively decrease as additional details transform what had been a sketch into a veritable blueprint for the good society.

To enumerate the particular details—the sufficient conditions—of a good society is effectively to prohibit individuality and social change. A planned society, a society in which sufficient conditions are politically determined and coercively imposed, is "closed" to the spontaneous innovations of free association. We see this in the utopian writings of Plato and his many admirers. A utopian society is a perfect society, one that has been carefully designed by a wise and beneficent lawgiver. Any deviation from perfection must necessarily be for the worse, so social change—which in this scheme is but another name for social degeneration—must be arrested at all costs. And this, in turn, requires the suppression of individuality. The individual's pursuit of happiness—that powerful and unpredictable agent of social change—must be subordinated for the sake of a good society, as specified in the utopian blueprint of sufficient conditions.

conflict b/t individual interests & collective plan

The difference between these models of political philosophy is reflected historically in two different meanings of the word "political." The Greek *polis*, from which our word "political" is derived, referred to many aspects of the ancient Greek city-state in addition to its government—to its religious, familial, and educational institutions, for example. Most Greek philosophers, most notably Aristotle, did not distinguish between the political and the social but used "political" to denote *all* kinds of institutions, whether coercive *or* voluntary. Thus, where Aristotle said that man is naturally a "political animal," later Aristotelians would sometimes substitute "social animal" or "social and political animal."

The older, more expansive meaning of "political," which included every kind of institution, tended to generate a theory of sufficient conditions. Over time, however, philosophers began to distinguish the political sphere of governmental coercion from the social sphere of voluntary interaction. It was during this development that philosophers adopted a more restrictive view of political philosophy as a theory of necessary conditions for a good society. The political sphere of coercion was now set apart from the social sphere of voluntary association, and it became a major task of political philosophy to establish a bright line between these two spheres. This was the perspective adopted by classical liberals. They agreed with John Milton's comment in *Areopagitica* (1644): "Here the great art lies, to discern in what the law is to bid restraint and punishment, and in what things persuasion only is to work."

milton

According to classical liberals, a theory of justice should define and delimit the proper sphere of government—the realm of legitimate coercion, in contradistinction to the social realm of voluntary interaction. A government should concern itself only with matters of justice, while leaving individuals free to pursue their own values in religious, economic, and personal affairs. This meant that the primary task of political philosophy, strictly speaking, is to determine the nature of a *just* society rather than a *good* society per se.

Adam Smith clearly expressed this distinction in *The Theory of Moral Sentiments* (1759; 6th ed., 1790), where he discussed "that remarkable distinction between justice and all the other social virtues." The obligations of justice "may be extorted by force," whereas the social virtues of beneficence—those affiliated with friendship, charity, generosity, and the like—should depend solely on "advice and persuasion." Indeed, "for equals to use force against one another" in an effort to compel the observance of social virtues other than justice "would be thought the highest degree of insolence and presumption."

Justice, according to Smith, is necessary for the very existence of society. Even if people interacted for no reason other than personal gain, narrowly conceived, a society that enforces the rules of justice could function satisfactorily. But a just society is not necessarily the best possible society. The moral quality of a just society will depend on the voluntary social virtues (which Smith subsumed under the label "beneficence") practiced by its members.

> Society may subsist among different men, as among different merchants, from a sense of its utility, without any mutual love or affection; and though no man in it should owe any obligation [apart from justice],

7

or be bound in gratitude to any other, it may still be upheld by a mercenary exchange of good offices according to an agreed valuation.

. . . Society may subsist, though not in the most comfortable state, without beneficence; but the prevalence of injustice must utterly destroy it. . . . [Beneficence] is the ornament which embellishes, not the foundation which supports the building, and which it was, therefore, sufficient to recommend, but by no means necessary to impose. Justice, on the contrary, is the main pillar that upholds the whole edifice. If it is removed, the great, the immense fabric of human society . . . must in a moment crumble into atoms.

From this libertarian perspective, political philosophy is concerned with the nature of a good society only insofar as it establishes conditions that are necessary, but not sufficient, for a good society. Political philosophy addresses the nature of a *just* society; whether the members of that society practice other moral virtues that render the society good rather than merely tolerable will depend on their voluntary decisions and actions. Those issues fall within the purview of ethics in the broadest sense; they are not matters of *political* philosophy per se.

Having laid this groundwork, I will now address an obvious and common objection to the libertarian conception of a just society: *How can justice be maintained in a society if most of its members lack the social virtues essential to a free society?* If, for example, most people are looking for any opportunity to cheat or rob others, and are restrained *only* by the fear of legal punishment, then the foundation of social order will be precarious indeed. If we are free to make our own decisions in pursuit of our own interests (so long as we respect the equal rights of others), then why would we ever respect the *moral* autonomy of others—their rights—except incidentally, as when we deem voluntary interaction conducive to our own ends or when we fear the legal consequences of aggression? Even if, as Adam Smith argued, a just society could exist without the social virtues of beneficence, what kind of society would it be? Would any reasonable person *really* want to live in that kind of society?

Problems like these underlie most arguments in favor of a government that does more than enforce the rules of justice, a government that also promotes social virtues through education, vice laws, and so forth. Every libertarian knows those

Liberty is the school of virtue

arguments, so I will not repeat them here. But we should understand how the traditional debates over self-interest have influenced this controversy. If, as Thomas Hobbes and some other philosophers maintained, self-interest is the sole motive of human action, then how can benevolence and other social virtues possibly arise in a free society in which the pursuit of self-interest is unfettered by laws that restrain immorality? What is the origin of our social passions, and to what extent can those passions hold our purely selfish inclinations in check? Why should we care about others unless their welfare is connected to our personal interests? Given human nature, is authentic benevolence even possible? If our natural disposition is to treat other people as means to our ends rather than as ends in themselves, then how can a free and spontaneous social order possibly sustain itself?

These and similar questions have occupied the attention of classical liberal philosophers for centuries. Indeed, entire books, such as Smith's *The Theory of Moral Sentiments*, were written to explain how the voluntary social virtues will arise in a free society, and how rational self-interest will actually strengthen the bonds of social order. Classical liberals tended to agree with John Milton (*The Second Defence of the English People*, 1654) that "liberty is the best school of virtue, and affords the strongest encouragement to the practice."

Virtue cannot be coercively imposed, nor can it be acquired by eliminating all possible sources of vice. As Milton wrote in *Areopagitica* (1644):

> What wisdom can there be to choose, what continence to forbear, without the knowledge of evil? He that can apprehend and consider vice with all her baits and seeming pleasures, and yet abstain, and yet distinguish, and yet prefer that which is truly better, he is the true warfaring Christian. I cannot praise a fugitive and cloistered virtue unexercised and unbreathed, that never sallies out and sees her adversary, but slinks out of the race, where that immoral garland is to be run for, not without dust and heat. Assuredly we bring not innocence into the world, we bring impurity much rather; that which purifies us is trial, and trial is by what is contrary. That virtue therefore which is but a youngling in the contemplation of evil, and knows not the utmost that vice promises to her followers, and rejects it, is but a blank virtue.

2

David Hume

I wish to begin my discussion of the Scottish philosopher David Hume (1711–1776) with some inside baseball. By this I mean how those modern libertarians influenced by Ayn Rand sometimes view Hume. Rand ranked Hume high on her list of intellectual villains, as we see in this passage from *For the New Intellectual: The Philosophy of Ayn Rand* (Random House, 1961):

> When Hume declared that he saw objects moving about, but never saw such a thing as "causality"—it was the voice of Attila that men were hearing. It was Attila's soul that spoke when Hume declared that he experienced a flow of fleeting states inside his skull such as sensations, feelings or memories, but had never caught the experience of such a *thing as consciousness or self.* When Hume declared that the

13

apparent existence of an object did not guarantee that it would not vanish spontaneously next moment, and the sunrise of today did not prove that the sun would rise tomorrow; when he declared that philosophical speculation was a game, like chess or hunting, of no significance whatever to the practical course of human existence, since reason proved that existence was unintelligible and only the ignorant maintained the illusion of knowledge—all of this accompanied by vehement opposition to the mysticism of the Witch Doctor and by protestations of loyalty to reason and science—what men were hearing was the manifesto of a philosophical move that can be designated only as *Attila-ism*.

Although I would not associate Hume's epistemology with Rand's literary ideal type of "Attila," and though I might disagree with Rand's characterization in other respects, I share her low estimation of Hume's theory of knowledge, which I regard as quite crude —as when Hume treats ideas as nothing more than "faint images" of "impressions" (i.e., perceptions). Although Hume's theory is sometimes represented as a continuation of Lockean empiricism, John Locke's careful analysis of abstractions in *An Essay Concerning Human*

Understanding (1690), which resembles Rand's approach in some respects, is far superior to anything found in Hume.

For Rand, a theory of knowledge is the sine qua non of a philosophy, the foundation that will profoundly affect one's theory of ethics, politics, and so forth. Consequently, those libertarians who accept Rand's approach tend to dismiss Hume out of hand, as if nothing he wrote could be of value. But, as many commentators have noted, there is a curious disconnect between Hume's epistemological skepticism and his moral and social philosophy. As Charles W. Hendel explained in his Introduction (1957) to Hume's *An Enquiry Concerning the Principles of Morals* (1752), "Hume was *not* skeptical in this work of moral philosophy." And Hendel continues:

> The first thing Hume insists upon against any skepticism in morality is "the reality of moral distinctions." They are real and they are important. They are not merely matters of convention or products of education. They originate naturally in the life of man in society.

Of the book referred to by Hendel, *An Enquiry Concerning the Principles of Morals* (which would become the second part of *Enquiries Concerning Human Understanding and Concerning the Principles of Morals*, 1777), Hume later said that it

Hume's Enquiry substantially different from Treatises?

was "of all my writings, historical, philosophical, or literary, incomparably my best." Scholars disagree over whether the later *Enquiry* is merely a briefer and more elegantly written version of Hume's earlier treatment of ethics in Book III of *A Treatise of Human Nature* (1739), or whether Hume changed his views somewhat in the later book. *A Treatise of Human Nature*, which is widely regarded as Hume's true masterpiece, was written while Hume was a young man and unknown in literary circles. After it "fell dead-born from the press," Hume resolved to write a more accessible version of the ideas contained in *A Treatise of Human Nature*, which can be quite difficult to read, and this led to his shorter *Enquiries*, an exemplar of how to write philosophy in an essay style.

elaborate / substantial change?

One thing is certain: in his later book on ethics, Hume avoided some of the controversial language and expressions that appear in the *Treatise*. For example, we find no references in the *Enquiry* to justice being an "artificial" virtue—an unfortunate choice of words in the *Treatise* that generated considerable misunderstanding among readers (for reasons I will explain presently). Moreover, some of Hume's hopped-up expressions in the *Treatise* do not appear in the *Enquiry*, most notably the infamous remark, "Reason is, and ought only to be the slave of the passions, and can never pretend to any other office than to serve and obey them." One can imagine a young

Hume being delighted with this striking bit of rhetoric, even though it could (and did) lead to misunderstandings about the points he wished to make in the *Treatise*. Hume was not the only young writer in the history of philosophy who was occasionally overexuberant.

F. A. Hayek was the chief conduit through which Hume's moral, political, and social theory entered the mainstream of modern libertarian thought. In his article "The Legal and Political Philosophy of David Hume" (originally presented as a lecture at the University of Freiburg on July 18, 1963), Hayek bemoaned the fact that Hume's legal and political philosophy had been "curiously neglected." In addition to being "one of the founders of economic theory" and the greatest British legal philosopher before Bentham, Hume "gives us probably the only comprehensive statement of the legal and political philosophy which later became known as [classical] liberalism." Although I think Hayek sometimes cast Hume's ideas in a more favorable light than they warrant, his article remains essential reading for libertarians who want to understand Hume's contributions to classical liberalism.

In this chapter (and the one that follows), I can do no more than sketch some of Hume's ideas in moral and social philosophy, especially as they pertain to self-interest, social order, and utility. First, however, I wish to clear up a controversy that I mentioned previously, namely, Hume's references, in _A Treatise of Human Nature_, to justice being an "artificial" virtue, or an "invention" (as he sometimes called it).

This language, which Hume later abandoned, provoked a good deal of criticism from his contemporaries, who claimed that Hume was attempting to overthrow a natural-law ethics in favor of moral subjectivism. But even in the _Treatise_, Hume made it clear that he had no such intention. (For an excellent discussion of this problem, see Stephen Buckle, _Natural Law and the Theory of Property: Grotius to Hume_, Oxford University Press, 1991.) As Hume wrote in _A Treatise of Human Nature_:

> To avoid giving offense, I must here observe, that when I deny justice to be a natural virtue, I make use of the word _natural_, only as opposed to _artificial_. In another sense of the word; as no principle of the human mind is more natural than a sense of virtue; so no virtue is more natural than justice. Mankind is an inventive species; and where an invention is obvious and absolutely necessary, it may as properly be said to be natural as any thing that proceeds immediately from original principles, without the intervention of thought or reflection. Though the rules of justice be _artificial_, they are not _arbitrary_. Nor is the expression

18

improper to call them *Laws of Nature*; if by natural ✶
we understand what is common to any species, or
even if we confine it to mean what is inseparable from
the species.

Justice, according to Hume, is not a natural sentiment of
human beings (such as the affection that a mother feels for
her child), nor is it an eternal truth discernible by reason   ✶
alone, independent of experience. Rather, justice is a social
phenomenon, one that emerges over time as people reflect
on how they benefit from social interaction and how those
benefits can be preserved.

To say that the rules of justice are not arbitrary is to say
that they cannot be altered or abolished by human will or
decree—a crucial tenet of the natural-law tradition. People
come to value justice as essential to society because it is *in fact*
essential to society. We come to formulate the rules of justice
after sufficient experience and reflection teach us their role in
preserving social order. Thus, in referring to the rules of justice
as "conventions," Hume meant that they must be discovered
over time, through the trial and error of circumstances, as
experience reveals their usefulness, or utility. The rules of
justice cannot be deduced from axiomatic premises by reason
alone; they depend on experience and on our analysis of that

experience, which teach us the indispensable role that justice plays in maintaining social order.

In order to appreciate what Hume was getting at, we need to know something about the tradition he opposed. There were two broad currents in British moral philosophy during the 18th century: One, as I explained in an essay on Anthony Ashley Cooper (1671–1713), the Third Earl of Shaftesbury, is "sentimentalism"—so called because of its focus on the role played by human sentiments (feelings, emotions, etc.) in human action, a role that must be appreciated if we are to understand why humans behave as they do and how social cooperation comes about.[1] The second current is commonly called "moral rationalism"—so-called because of its claim that justice and other moral principles can be derived and justified by reason *alone*.

Moral rationalism was the target of Hume's critical analysis of reason in moral philosophy, and of his celebrated Is–Ought dichotomy. Moral rationalists, said Hume, defend "an abstract theory of morals" and pretend "to found everything on reason," while ignoring the role of sentiments and passions in the evolution of institutions, such as property. According to moral rationalism, our notions of virtue and vice, right and wrong, justice and injustice, have their origin in reason alone,

20

[handwritten margin note: moral realists: moral necessity like mathematical necessity]

in the same way that our scientific and mathematical notions originate in reason. Our practical knowledge of ethics, like the theoretical knowledge of mathematics, can be logically demonstrated, according to rationalists; both are based on the "eternal and unalterable relations" of their respective subject matters. Moral obligation, in this view, is a species of rational obligation. Just as we are constrained to accept mathematical propositions when their truth becomes evident to the mind, so we are similarly constrained to accept ethical prescriptions.

The approach to which Hume objected is found in the writings of Samuel Clarke, a well-known philosopher and theologian of the time. (Another rationalist was William Wollaston, an influential 18th-century philosopher specifically mentioned by Hume.) According to Clarke (*Discourse upon Natural Religion*, 1706), there is a Rule of Equity stating that "we so deal with every Man, as in like Circumstances, we could reasonably expect he should deal with Us." The human understanding naturally submits to a demonstrated truth. It is not a matter of will, for example, whether we believe that twice two equals four. Once we clearly understand what numbers mean and how they are related mathematically, we have no choice but to accept the proposition "$2 + 2 = 4$" as necessarily true. Similarly, once we understand the nature

[handwritten margin note: Clarke's Rule of Equity]

of human beings and their social relationships, we have no choice but to accept the truth of basic moral propositions, such as the Rule of Equity. Quoting Clarke:

> For, as the addition of certain numbers, necessarily produces a certain sum . . . so in moral matters, there are certain necessary and unalterable respects or relations of things, which have not their original from arbitrary and positive constitution, but are of eternal necessity in their own nature.

The following argument by Clarke was typical of moral rationalists:

> The reason which obliges every man in practice, so to deal always with another, as he would reasonably expect that others should in like circumstances deal with him, is the very same, as that which forces him in speculation to affirm, that if one line or number be equal to another, that other is reciprocally equal to it. Iniquity is the very same in action, as falsity or contradiction in theory, and the same cause which makes one absurd, makes the other unreasonable. Whatever relation or proportion one man in any case bears to another, the same that other, when put in

like circumstances, bears to him. Whatever I judge reasonable or unreasonable for another to do for me, that, by the same judgment, I declare reasonable or unreasonable, that I in the like case should do for him. And to deny this in either word or action, is as if a man should contend, that, though two and three are equal to five, yet five are not equal to two and three.

It was in reaction to his kind of hyper-rationalism that the sentimentalists, such as Shaftesbury, Hume, and Adam Smith, proposed an alternate psychological and sociological theory of justice, one that took into account the role of human passions in the genesis of moral principles and social institutions, such as private property. I will examine this approach, as developed by Hume, in the next chapter.

3

David Hume on Justice

Why is society advantageous to man? Because, said David Hume, we require for our survival and well-being many things that we cannot easily (if at all) provide for ourselves but that require the cooperation of others. Three factors are primarily responsible for the benefits of social cooperation. First, the division of labor increases the productive capacity of society beyond that which could be achieved separately by its members. Second, specialization enables us to improve our skills beyond what would be possible in a solitary state. Third, society provides a remedy in times of emergency, as when illness or a natural disaster leaves us destitute. In society, such emergencies will bring friends and family to our aid, whereas they would probably cause our death in a solitary condition.

[handwritten: How do ppl. learn of the benefits of social order — 1st from family]

Society therefore helps us in three basic ways. First, it combines and coordinates the labor of many people and thereby increases our own economic power. Second, it enhances our personal abilities by permitting us to concentrate on a specialized area. Third, it vastly improves our security by providing various sources of support and assistance during emergencies. "'Tis by this additional *force*, *ability*, and *security* that society becomes advantageous."

The mere existence of these benefits is not enough, however—people must become aware of *why* they are advantageous if those benefits are to be sustained in the long run. And this knowledge could not have been attained through reason alone. Why? Because the beneficial consequences of social cooperation are "remote and obscure" rather than immediately obvious. So how was this knowledge first acquired? Here Hume pointed to "that natural appetite betwixt the sexes" as the preeminent cause of the habit of social cooperation. Our natural sexual impulses, by producing children, create the miniature society of family members. The parents are stronger than their offspring, and so are able to enforce their wills; but they also have a natural affection for their children, which causes them to moderate their power. Meanwhile, as children grow

[handwritten margin: model of the family as learning about benefits of social order]

But how do we go from interested benevolence
toward him to impartial justice toward strangers

up in their familial society, they come to understand and appreciate the benefits of social cooperation. They acquire the social habits, skills, and temperament that will render them fit to cooperate with strangers and others beyond their immediate family.

The crucial difference between a family and a larger society is that in the latter we must interact with strangers, people for whom we feel no natural affection. Hence our natural benevolence toward family and friends cannot account for the sentiment of justice, which requires impartiality above all else. Justice does not allow favoritism; it does not permit us to treat people we like differently from people we dislike. This is why our natural feelings of benevolence cannot account for the impartial sentiment of justice: benevolence is always partial, causing us to favor some people over others. How, then, can we explain the social evolution of justice? How can we account for this *disinterested* sentiment, given that man's natural social sentiments are biased in favor of himself and his inner circle of family and friends?

It was while addressing this question that Hume mentioned three kinds of goods that are possessed by human beings: the internal satisfaction of our minds, such as happiness; (A) the external advantages of our body, such as health; and the (B)

(Partial)
Selfishness, insecurity, scarcity

material possessions we have acquired through industry and good fortune.

The first category of goods, those pertaining to internal satisfaction, cannot be taken from us. The second, our physical capabilities and condition, can indeed be damaged or destroyed by another person, but the aggressor can gain nothing for himself by doing so. But the case is different with the third species of goods, our material possessions.

> [Our possessions] alone are both exposed to the violence of others, and may be transferred without suffering any loss or alteration; while at the same time, there is not a sufficient quantity of them to supply every one's desires and necessities. As the improvement, therefore, of these goods is the chief advantage of society, so the *instability* of their possession, along with their *scarcity*, is the chief impediment.

Property would be insecure in a state of nature, and it is in vain, said Hume, to expect a remedy for this inconvenience from man's uncultivated nature, which is dominated by his natural passions. As noted previously, people will naturally value their own welfare and the welfare of their inner circle (family and friends) over that of other members of society, so our natural affections are inconsistent with the sentiment of justice. Rather than cultivate a concern for strangers, our partial passion of self-interest will tend to strengthen the value we place on ourselves and on our inner circle at the expense of everyone else.

This is what Hume meant when he said that justice is not a "natural" virtue. We are not naturally inclined to value everyone equally, without showing favoritism to self, family, and friends—but this is exactly what the virtue of justice requires. What nature fails to provide, however, is compensated for by our judgment and understanding. As we become aware of the advantages of social cooperation, we also become aware of the need for security in our external possessions.

> This can be done after no other manner, than by a convention entered into by all the members of society to bestow stability on the possession of those external goods, and leave every one in the peaceable enjoyment of what he may acquire by his fortune and industry. By this means, every one knows what he may safely possess; and the passions are restrained in their partial and contradictory motions. Nor is such a restraint contrary to these passions; for if so, it could never be entered into, nor maintained; but it is only

conventions of property are incentive compatible

contrary to their heedless and impetuous movement. Instead of departing from our own interest, or from that of our nearest friends, by abstaining from the possessions of others, we cannot better consult both these interests, than by such a convention; because it is by that means we maintain society, which is so necessary to their well-being and subsistence, as well as to our own.

Hume stressed that the "convention" of respecting property rights does not arise from a contract among members of society. Rather, it arises from a sense of common interest that induces people to regulate their conduct by certain rules. I observe that it is in my interest to respect the property rights of another person, provided he respects mine. And he is also aware of the advantage to be gained from this reciprocity. Therefore, as we each become aware of the advantages of reciprocity, we adjust our behavior accordingly, without ever consulting each other or making an explicit pact wherein we exchange promises.

There is, Hume conceded, a kind of agreement involved in this social convention, but it does not involve mutual promises. My actions are taken with a view to your actions and are predicated on the expectation that you will behave in a certain way. But I never promise you that I will act in a certain manner, nor do you promise me. Hume compared this *rowing a boat* situation to two men rowing a boat. Each man exerts labor on the supposition that the other man will do likewise, and each adjusts his movements to the movements of the other—but all of this occurs without an exchange of promises or an explicit agreement between the two men. The cooperation is spontaneous and implicitly understood, not planned in advance and expressed in promises or a contract.

Property rights, therefore, arise over time, as people become sensible of the need for security, and as they become aware that this security can best be achieved by respecting the property rights of everyone in society. And this occurs without any exchange of promises. The institution of property is largely a spontaneous product of self-interested behavior. No ancient lawgiver, such as Moses or Lycurgus or Solon, figured out the advantages of private property and bestowed the necessary laws for protecting them on the rest of humanity. Property rights—like language and money—evolved over time and were established as conventions, as people came to respect them routinely, as a matter of habit.

Hume's account is especially significant for classical liberal ideology because of its stress on the fusion of self-interest and public utility through property rights, which is the institutional manifestation of justice. As with many British moralists, Hume treated self-interest as a natural sentiment, an inherent disposition in human nature, that can lead to either good or bad consequences, depending on how it is managed and directed by reason.

Justice forbids us to interfere with the property rights of others, and, when such rights are secure, "there remains little or nothing to be done towards settling a perfect harmony and concord" in society. Social harmony cannot be achieved, however, so long as man's natural passions, which give "preference to ourselves and friends, above strangers," are "not restrained by any convention or agreement." Our partial self-interest, if unrestrained by reason, generates the anti-social passion of avidity—the desire to acquire goods and possessions for ourselves and our nearest friends. Avidity is "insatiable, perpetual, universal, and directly destructive of society," so this passion must be regulated or checked. But benevolence toward strangers is too weak to "counter-balance the love of gain," as are other passions not linked to self-interest. This leaves only self-interest itself, rightly understood, to counteract the undesirable consequences of a partial self-interest, narrowly conceived. We moderate our self-interested passions as we come to understand the long-range benefits of social cooperation.

> There is no passion, therefore, capable of controlling the interested affection, but the very affection itself, by an alteration of its direction. Now this alteration must necessarily take place upon the least reflection; since 'tis evident, that the passion is much better satisfy'd by its restraint, than by its liberty, and that by preserving society, we make much greater advances in the acquiring possessions, than by running into the solitary and forlorn conditions, which must follow upon violence and an universal licence.

conventions make our passions compatible by directing them into certain patterns

restraint for greater riches of society

That self-interest must restrain and regulate itself leads to an interesting observation about its moral status. Whether self-interest be deemed virtuous or vicious has no bearing whatever on the origin of society, according to Hume. Whether we view man's social nature as arising from his virtues or vices does not alter the fact that the self-interested passions are too strong to be checked by anything other than themselves. The key issue, therefore, does not concern the goodness or wickedness of human nature, "but the degrees of men's sagacity or folly."

The self-interested passion of avidity restrains itself by the establishment of property rights—a "rule for the stability of possessions." Nothing is more "simple and obvious" than the need for this rule. Every parent understands its role in maintaining peace among his children, and it will quickly improve as the society becomes larger. Hume therefore dismissed the possibility that men could long remain in "that savage condition, which precedes society." On the contrary, "his very first state and situation may justly be esteem'd social." The supposed pre-social state of nature—that Hobbesian condition of perpetual strife—is a philosophical fiction, an abstraction that never did, nor ever could, exist in reality. It is a hypothetical model concocted by philosophers in which the two principal parts of human nature—the affections and the understanding—are mentally separated, and the former considered in isolation from the latter. To imagine human beings as being driven solely by their affections without any direction from their understanding is necessarily to incapacitate them for social life.

In short, according to Hume, the rules of justice are "artificial," in the sense that they do not spring naturally from innate sentiments and dispositions. Instead, the rules of justice emerge as we reason about the lessons of experience, which teach us that justice is an indispensable condition for social order and harmony. Justice cannot be deduced from the nature of rational beings alone, as moral rationalists maintained. We must also take into account the nonrational features of human nature, such as our natural sentiments, and the external conditions in which people find themselves, such as the requirements imposed by economic scarcity.

4

Thomas Hobbes

Elsewhere, I have written the following about Anthony Ashley Cooper (1671–1713), the Third Earl of Shaftesbury:

> He was especially critical of a doctrine known as *psychological egoism*, which insisted that all human actions are necessarily self-interested. In one respect Shaftesbury did not object to this primitive hedonistic analysis, since all human action is motivated by the desire to attain happiness, or satisfaction of the self, in *some* sense. Nevertheless, it is a serious error to suppose that *all* human actions are motivated by self-interest, as that term is commonly understood.

"Psychological egoism" is a modern label; during the 18th century, David Hume and others frequently called the same idea "the selfish system." This is the doctrine that all human actions, however other-regarding or disinterested they may seem, are in fact motivated by considerations of self-interest. (There is also a theory known as "psychological hedonism," according to which all actions are motivated by the desire for pleasure, or personal satisfaction, but I will ignore that approach for now.)

Those leading 18th-century philosophers who criticized psychological egoism (e.g., Shaftesbury, Francis Hutcheson, Joseph Butler, David Hume, and Adam Smith) were typically classical liberals who wished to rebut the theories of Thomas Hobbes (1588–1679), especially as explained in his masterpiece, *Leviathan* (1651). Hobbes, according to his liberal critics, had parlayed psychological egoism into a defense of absolute sovereignty, along with the corollary doctrine that individuals must surrender their rights and obey an absolute government unconditionally in order to maintain social order. Thus, by attacking psychological egoism, Hobbes's critics hoped to undermine his defense of absolutism at its root.

So what is the relationship between psychological egoism and political absolutism? I will consider this issue presently, but first I should call attention to a possible glitch. According to some modern Hobbesian scholars, Hobbes was not a psychological egoist at all. Contrary to the many critics who linked him to the "selfish system," Hobbes did not in fact believe that every motive can ultimately be reduced to self-interest. An able defender of this interpretation was the moral philosopher Bernard Gert. In his introduction to *Man and Citizen* (translations of two early works by Hobbes, *De Homine* and *De Cive*), published in 1972 by Anchor Books), Gert argued that the Hobbesian approach "is not psychological egoism." Rather, Hobbes merely argued that other-regarding motives, such as benevolence, play a minor role in human affairs. Their influence is "limited and cannot be used as a foundation upon which to build a state."

This is not the place for me to debate this issue, even if I were inclined to do so, except to note that many passages by Hobbes definitely point in the direction of psychological egoism, whereas others seem to support Gert's interpretation. Suffice it to say that Hobbes, who was a bear for consistency in philosophical reasoning, did not always practice what he preached.

In the final analysis it doesn't matter much if Hobbes was a strict psychological egoist, for the essential points made by his liberal critics would still apply either way. His psychological theories were quite crude in any case, even by 17th-century standards, and they sometimes give the appearance of having been concocted ad hoc, as a rationale for vesting absolute power in a state.

Hobbes: Social motivations boil down to honour (vanity) & profit

Now, let's take a look at some of the ideas defended by Hobbes that so alarmed his liberal critics and caused them to criticize psychological egoism, sometimes in considerable detail.

In *De Cive* (*The Citizen*, 1642), Hobbes denied the common maxim that man is naturally a social animal. Man does not desire social interaction for its own sake (i.e., because such interaction is inherently desirable or pleasurable) but because of the personal advantages he hopes to acquire. These gains are both material and psychological. In addition to the desire to profit from commerce and the like, which is motivated largely by our jealousy toward those who possess more than we do, social interaction also caters to our vanity, as we revel in the attention, praise, and esteem we receive from others.

Hobbes's cynical view of human nature is painfully evident throughout his writings, and to reinforce and illustrate this cynicism Hobbes sometimes invited readers to imagine themselves in certain situations. Suppose you are at a social gathering. Your primary reason for participating in a conversation will be to get something from others or to puff yourself up; you will hope to "receive some honor or profit from it." You may, for example, attempt to stand out by telling a funny story, often at the expense of someone else. Friends who are not present may have "their whole life, sayings, [and] actions . . . examined, judged, condemned." Even participants who leave the gathering early may be the butt of sarcasm and ridicule, and all this for no reason other than to amuse their supposed friends. "And these are indeed the true delights of society," according to Hobbes.

Hobbes was a witty fellow, but however humorous these and similar observations may be, it would be a mistake to dismiss them as mere witticisms. When Hobbes talked about the vanity inherent in human nature, he was making a serious point with serious implications. As he put it, "All society [i.e., all social interaction] therefore is either for gain, or for glory; that is, not so much for love of our fellows, as for the love of ourselves." But no society can subsist if these selfish motives are permitted to operate unchecked. In a state of nature (a society without government), people would exploit others mercilessly, even to the point of murdering innocent people for their property, and the only remedy for this war of all against all is *fear*.

People will naturally pursue any goals that they regard as conducive to their own good, however much their selfish actions may harm others. Only fear—a counteracting self-interested motive—can persuade people to change the direction of their normal self-interested actions. Only the self-interested incentive of fear, especially the fear of death, can overpower our desire to exploit others by violent means, because we value our own lives more than we value the goods that violence may yield. This is

violence for gain

the basic rationale for a government with absolute power; only such a government can instill the continuous fear, including the fear of death, necessary to maintain social order. There are no other sentiments or dispositions, such as benevolence, sympathy, or a regard for justice, that can possibly override our selfish proclivities and sustain a *voluntary* social order. Thus an absolute government, one that enforces unwavering obedience by instilling perpetual fear among its citizens, is a necessary precondition of social order and internal peace.

Hobbes expanded on this theme in *Leviathan*. The following passage (from chapter XIII) is typical. After asserting that men are roughly equal in their physical and mental abilities, such that a single person, no matter how strong or smart, always has something to fear from others, Hobbes continued:

> From this equality of ability, ariseth equality of hope in the attaining of our Ends. And therefore if any two men desire the same thing, which nevertheless they cannot both enjoy, they become enemies; and in the way to their End (which is principally their own conservation, and sometimes their delectation only) endeavour to destroy, or subdue one an other. And from hence it comes to passe, that where an Invader hath no more to feare, than an other man's

single power; if one plant, sow, build, or possesse a convenient Seat, others may probably be expected to come prepared with forces united, to dispossess, and deprive him, not only of the fruit of his labour, but also of his life, or liberty. And the Invader again is in the like danger of another.

A little later in the same chapter, Hobbes identified a psychological factor that supposedly will cause conflict with our fellows unless we are all rendered afraid by a supervening power. We want others to value us as much as we value ourselves; and when they don't, we get offended and angry—emotions that will lead to violent conflict and even to murder. This argument, though full of obvious holes, Hobbes presented with his typical self-assurance, as if he were making a profound and airtight point. (Contrary to many modern philosophers, I have a rather low opinion of Hobbes' philosophical arguments and his supposed rigor.)

Againe, men have no pleasure, (but on the contrary a great deale of griefe) in keeping company, where there is no power able to over-awe them all. For every man looketh that his companion should value him, at the same rate he sets upon himselfe: And upon all signs of contempt, or undervaluing, naturally endeavours,

43

as far as he dares (which amongst them that have no common power to keep them quiet, is far enough to make them destroy each other) to extort a greater value from his contemners, by dommage [i.e., injury]; and from others, by the example.

Given the innate dispositions of human nature that will supposedly generate a perpetual war of every man against every man in a state of nature, we might wonder if Hobbes was aware of how rational human beings can resolve their conflicts and agree to cooperate for the benefit of everyone concerned. Well, Hobbes was well aware of this possibility, and he discussed the fundamental principles of social order in chapters XIV and XV of *Leviathan*. His second Fundamental Law of Nature (by "Laws of Nature" Hobbes meant normative principles that will further peace and social order) reads as follows:

From this [first] Fundamentall Law of Nature, by which men are commanded to endeavour Peace, is derived this second Law; *That a man be willing, when others are so too, as farre-forth, as for Peace, and defence of himselfe he shall think it necessary, to lay down the right to all things [in a state of nature]; and be contented with so much liberty against other men, as he would allow other men against himselfe.* . . . If other men will not

lay down their Right, as well as he; then there is no
Reason for any one to divest himselfe of his: For that
would be to expose himself to Prey.

This brings us to the Hobbesian version of the social contract. I cannot adequately cover this complicated notion here,
but I will mention a few points that relate to Hobbes's defense
of absolutism.

The first point may seem to split hairs, but it is important
to an understanding of Hobbes's theory. To refer to a "social
contract" may be a bit misleading when speaking of Hobbes;
more precise is the term "social *covenant*."

A covenant, for Hobbes, is a type of contract, one that
involves future performance. A contract is "the mutual trans-
ferring of right." For example, if I sell you my car for $5,000,
I agree to transfer the legal right (or title) to my car in
exchange for the legal right to your money. This exchange of
rights is the essence of contract. But there are different kinds
of contract. Suppose I deliver my car with the understanding
you will pay $5,000 after three months. Here I execute my
part of the bargain immediately, while trusting you to fulfill
your part of the bargain in the future. Hobbes called this kind
of contract—a contract that involves a future performance by
at least one of the parties—a "covenant," or "pact."

Hobbes w/o absolute state, there can be no cooperation (All PD)

According to Hobbes, the reciprocal agreement citizens enter into to deal with one another by peaceful means is a social covenant. It is a covenant wherein citizens rely on the future performance of other citizens. Such covenants involve serious and ultimately fatal problems if made in a state of nature because, motivated by self-interest, the person who has not yet fulfilled his side of the agreement will almost always renege on his promise. (Hobbes seemed blissfully unaware of the power of unwritten customs and social sanctions that do not involve a government.) Without a government to compel the future performance of other parties, it would be irrational for a person to enter into covenants at all, because his trust in the other party is bound to prove unwarranted. Indeed, according to Hobbes, covenants made in a state of nature are not even morally binding. Only the fear of governmental punishment for violating a covenant can make covenants rational, and therefore morally binding.

Hobbes doesn't have theory of cooperation w/o fear of state

This is the basic reasoning behind the Hobbesian defense of absolute government. Unless self-interested individuals fear being punished for their violations of agreements, such agreements will be impossible, and there will exist no foundation for social order. Hobbes makes no allowance for the possibility that contracting parties will fulfill their agreements as a matter of honor or from a sense of justice. Indeed, these options

① do this b/c absolute state is a magic exogenous that overcomes the problem of PD?

would not even be rational in a state of nature, because the naïve party would leave himself open to being exploited by others, and this would not be in his self-interest.

The reciprocal agreement in the Hobbesian social covenant consists of everyone (except the sovereign) renouncing his right to pursue self-interested actions as he deems fit. But there is no contract (or agreement of any kind) between the sovereign and the citizens in this tortuous hypothetical scheme. Citizens do not transfer or delegate any rights to the sovereign. Rather, they agree to *renounce* their rights, provided others agree, and this social covenant is then enforced by the sovereign, who retains the same fundamental right (to do whatever he likes, in effect) that he possessed in the state of nature. In other words, after the social covenant occurs, the sovereign is left with complete discretion in deciding what to do with the citizens. The citizens, in contrast, having renounced all their rights (with the sole exception of the right of self-preservation, which is inalienable, even for Hobbes), have no right to disobey or even to question the sovereign, who remains in a state of nature vis-à-vis the citizens. And those (virtually) rightless beings certainly don't possess the rights of resistance and revolution, regardless of how unjust or tyrannical the sovereign may be. On the contrary, justice itself has no meaning apart from the will of the sovereign. Whatever the sovereign decrees is just, by definition.

We can now understand why Hobbes painted a terrifying picture of a society without government. If people are to submit unconditionally to an absolute ruler, their only alternative—a state of nature—must be sufficiently horrible to justify this drastic measure. Hobbes admitted that men will agree to the social covenant from fear alone, specifically, the fear of death in a war of all against all. But covenants motivated by fear, he insisted, are still binding.

I have presented this summary so that readers unfamiliar with Hobbes will appreciate why so many liberal philosophers targeted him for attack. Although Hobbes did not spawn many disciples per se, parts of his analysis found their way into the writings of other important philosophers, as we see in the work of Samuel Pufendorf (1632–1694) on international law. (We even find some aspects of the Hobbesian approach to self-interest in the libertarian classic *Cato's Letters*, by John Trenchard and Thomas Gordon, 1720–1723.) Some key Hobbesian ideas influenced later sociological thinking, as we see in the work of Ferdinand Tönnies (1855–1936); and Hobbesian elements are evident in some modern economic theories. (Those economists who invoke Hobbes frequently show little understanding of his ideas.) As I noted at the beginning of this chapter, liberal philosophers thought it necessary to attack not only Hobbes's political conclusions but also the premises on which he built those conclusions. Chief among those premises was the Hobbesian notion of self-interest and how that supposedly ubiquitous motive renders social order impossible unless it is severely restrained by the fear of an absolute government. I discuss some of those criticisms, especially as they pertain to psychological egoism, in the next chapter.

5

The Selfish System

Given Nathaniel Branden's still fairly recent death (December 3, 2014), it is fitting to begin this discussion of psychological egoism—or "the selfish system," as it was called in earlier centuries—by referring to an article on this topic that Branden wrote for *The Objectivist Newsletter* (September 1962). In "Isn't Everyone Selfish?" Branden stated the basic thesis of psychological egoism as follows: "Since every purposeful action is motivated by some value or goal that the actor desires, one always acts *selfishly*, whether one knows it or not."

Branden had a remarkable ability to analyze philosophical and psychological issues in clear and concise terms, as we see in his treatment of psychological egoism. Near the end of his article, Branden hit the nail on the head.

> The basic fallacy in the "everyone is selfish" argument consists of an extraordinarily crude equivocation. It is a psychological truism—a tautology—that all purposeful behavior is motivated. But to equate "*motivated* behavior" with "*selfish* behavior" is to blank out the distinction between an elementary fact of human psychology and the phenomenon of *ethical choice*. It is to evade the central problem of ethics, namely: By *what* is man to be motivated?

This type of criticism by no means originated with Branden; on the contrary, similar criticisms go back at least to the early 18th century, as I pointed out with regard to Shaftesbury in the previous chapter. And, as I explained in that chapter, classical liberals were especially concerned to rebut psychological egoism, because they associated it with the political teachings of Thomas Hobbes, who used it to buttress his case for absolute sovereignty. If we are necessarily motivated by self-interest, if we lack any natural sympathy for others and will observe the rules of justice only so long as those rules serve our own subjective interests, then we need a strong government to instill *fear* in citizens—a fear that will override our other self-interested concerns—if we are to attain even a minimal degree of social order. According to Hobbes, without the fear instilled by an absolute sovereign, we will lapse into the horrific state of nature, a condition of perpetual war of every man against every man where life is "nasty, brutish, and short."

Eighteenth-century British philosophers—or the "British Moralists," as they came to be known—criticized psychological egoism for more than political reasons. A substantial portion of their writings was concerned as much with what we now call psychology as with philosophy per se, as we now understand that term. They subsumed all investigations of human action, both prescriptive and descriptive, under the label "moral philosophy" or "moral science"—where "moral" pertained to three fundamental features of human nature: reason, volition, and purposeful behavior. These characteristics, they believed, distinguish human beings from other animals, so it is crucial to understand these features and their interrelationships if we are to understand "the springs of human action" (to use a phrase from David Hume). This type of investigation, they further believed, is indispensable if we are to understand the foundation and conditions of social order. Although the British Moralists disagreed among themselves on some issues, they unanimously rejected the Hobbesian argument that fear, and fear alone, can motivate people to interact peacefully. If a government restricts its coercive activities to enforcing the equal rights and freedoms of its citizens, then within that framework people will be motivated not only by self-interest but also by benevolence, justice, and other nonselfish factors—and this mix of motives will generate a desirable social order.

Now let's return to the particulars of psychological egoism. According to Branden, this doctrine conflates *motivated* actions with *self-interested* actions. To put this another way: it is obvious that we must be *interested* in *x* before we will act to achieve *x*; otherwise, we would lack any motive to pursue *x*. But to say that we must be interested in *x*, in *some* sense, before we will pursue *x* does not tell us *why* we are interested in *x*. We may be interested in *x* because we believe it will further our own interests, or we may be interested in *x* because we believe it will promote the welfare of another person, or (as we shall see in the arguments of Bishop Butler, which I discuss in the next chapter) we may be interested in *x* without either of these objectives in view.

Some early critics of psychological egoism claimed that it ultimately rests on a linguistic confusion that conflates "interested" with "self-interested." For example, the Scottish philosopher and sociologist Adam Ferguson (*An Essay on the*

History of Civil Society, 1767) wrote that "this supposed selfish philosophy," while masquerading as a significant insight into human nature, is actually nothing more than an "obtrusion of a mere innovation in language." Ordinary people use conventional language to distinguish between different types of motives: "Of this kind are the terms *benevolence* and *selfishness*, by which they express their desire of the welfare of others, or the care of their own." But then along comes the "speculative" philosopher who reshuffles the meanings of ordinary words and proudly announces his discovery that all human actions, including those that appear self-sacrificial, are ultimately selfish. In fact, however, that philosopher has merely "given us the appearance of something new, without any prospect of real advantage."

"The term *benevolent*," Ferguson continued, "is not employed to characterise persons who have no desires of their own, but persons whose own desires prompt them to procure the welfare of others." True, my desire to help others is *my* desire, and any attempt to satisfy that desire is an attempt to satisfy *my* desire—all this is quite tautological—but to say that I desire *x* does not tell us the *object*, or *goal*, of my desire, which may be to help others.

If we accept the reasoning of psychological egoism and equate my desires per se with self-interested desires and

(1) all humans are deceitful

thereby reduce *all* motives to self-interested motives, then, as Ferguson pointed out, we will need "a fresh supply of language, instead of that which by this seeming discovery we should have lost, in order to make the reasonings of men proceed as they formerly did." We simply could not communicate accurately with others unless we differentiated some kinds of motives from others; we need "different names to distinguish the humane from the cruel, and the benevolent from the selfish." The supposed discovery of the psychological egoist, to the effect that all motives are ultimately selfish motives, amounts to nothing more than a linguistic coup.

two kinds of selfish system (1)

David Hume, in "Of Self-Love" (Appendix II of *An Enquiry Concerning the Principles of Morals*), identified two versions of the selfish system. The first and least interesting is a type of cynicism that views all humans as corrupt and deceitful to some degree or another. Thus, when we appear or claim to be acting without a regard for our own interests, we are acting under false pretenses. If we donate liberally to charitable causes, this is not because we really care about anyone other than ourselves. Rather, we are attempting to make ourselves look good in the eyes of others, perhaps to win their praise and esteem.

The second version of the selfish system of morals is more complex philosophically. Hume described this theory as follows:

> There is another principle, somewhat resembling the former; which has been much insisted on by philosophers, and has been the foundation of many a system; that, whatever affection one may feel, or imagine he feels for others, no passion is, or can be disinterested; that the most generous friendship, however sincere, is a modification of self-love; and that, even unknown to ourselves, we seek only our own gratification, while we appear the most deeply engaged in schemes for the liberty and happiness of mankind. By a turn of imagination, by a refinement of reflection, by an enthusiasm of passion, we seem to take part in the interests of others, and imagine ourselves divested of all selfish considerations: but, at bottom, the most generous patriot and most niggardly miser, the bravest hero and most abject coward, have, in every action, an equal regard to their own happiness and welfare.

This version of psychological egoism does not deny that people sincerely believe that they are acting benevolently, without regard for their own interests. It does not dismiss all such claims as deceitful, self-serving pretense. Rather, it resorts to "a philosophical chemistry" that, by analyzing other-regarding motives into their true elements, teaches us that *every* action can be reduced to self-interest. A concern for oneself is the ubiquitous motive that has been "twisted and moulded, by a particular turn of imagination, into a variety of appearances."

This is the type of psychological egoism that was commonly attributed to Hobbes, as when he defined "pity" as "fear for oneself at the sight of another's distress." No matter how disinterested or other-regarding our passions may seem to be, the philosophical chemist, through a rigorous analysis of our passions and motives, is able to uncover their true foundation in self-interest.

Hume gave several interesting objections to this kind of analysis. Our distinctions between other-regarding dispositions, such as benevolence and generosity, and our selfish passions are based on "common language and observation," so they have a strong presumption in their favor. This presumption can be defeated only if some hypothesis is presented which, "by penetrating deeper into human nature," is able to prove how our other-regarding passions are nothing but modifications of our selfish passions. But all such demonstrations "have hitherto proved fruitless," having been refuted many times by earlier philosophers. (Although Hume did not mention Hobbes in this context, it was commonly—and correctly—said that Hobbes achieved his resolution of all motives into self-interested motives through arbitrary definitions.)

Given the repeated failures of the philosophical chemistry discussed by Hume, why did this enterprise prove so attractive to philosophers? Hume suggested that "love of *simplicity*" was largely to blame. Here Hume was thinking of the Newtonian system (or the Galilean system, in Hobbes's case), which had been able to explain diverse natural phenomena in terms of a few basic principles. But, according to Hume, this method of simplification, though indispensable in physics, should not be applied uncritically to human action. When exploring human passions, our personal experiences of those passions are likely to yield the most reliable results; and any attempt to "reduce all the various emotions to a perfect simplicity" is bound to lead us astray. When a philosopher attempts to explain emotions by referring to "some very intricate and refined" theory, we have good reason "to be extremely on our guard against so fallacious an hypothesis."

After these preliminary methodological remarks, Hume proceeded to consider the possibility that humans can act from "a disinterested benevolence." His points are essentially a summary of the ideas of Bishop Butler, a philosopher and theologian whom Hume admired and whose highly influential treatment of psychological egoism (and human motives generally) was the gold standard for the British Moralists. I explore the psychological theories of that remarkable philosopher in the next chapter.

6

Joseph Butler

Joseph Butler (1692–1752)—better known as Bishop Butler—was born into a Presbyterian family in Wantage (in the county of Berkshire), England. He enrolled in one of the many dissenting academies—private institutions that provided a university education for Protestant dissenters from the Established Church of England—and remained there until age 23. Around that time (in 1715) Butler converted to the Anglican faith and entered Oriel College, Oxford, to study for holy orders. He found the intellectual life at Oxford stifling—"Our people here," he wrote to the Newtonian philosopher Samuel Clarke, "never had any doubt in their lives concerning a received opinion; so that I cannot mention a difficulty to them"— but he stuck it out and graduated in 1718. Not long afterward he was ordained deacon, then priest, and was appointed preacher at the Rolls Chapel, in London. Butler was consecrated Bishop of Bristol in 1738.

It was while preaching at the Rolls Chapel that Butler delivered his *Fifteen Sermons on Human Nature*, which were published in 1726. (A second edition followed in 1729). It is in these *Sermons* that we find Butler's celebrated refutation of psychological egoism. (See the previous chapter for an explanation of this doctrine.) Although Butler was not a classical liberal, his extensive exploration of the relationship between "self-love" and "benevolence" influenced many 18th-century liberal philosophers. A case in point is David Hume, who, despite his religious skepticism, admired Butler—and not only for his *Sermons*. Hume also respected Butler's *Analogy of Religion* (1736), the most famous critique of deism ever written from a Christian perspective. As Ernest Campbell Mossner wrote in *The Life of David Hume* (1954, p. 110): "The *Analogy* was to remain the one theological work of the century that Hume was to deem worthy of serious consideration and whose author was always to be highly respected by him."

Eighteenth-century philosophers were not alone in praising Butler's treatment of psychological egoism; we find the same esteem expressed by modern philosophers.

For example, according to the English philosopher C. D. Broad, psychological egoism "was killed by Butler." Broad continued:

> [Butler] killed the theory so thoroughly that he sometimes seems to the modern reader to be flogging dead horses. Still, all good fallacies go to America when they die, and rise again as the latest discoveries of the local professors. So it will always be useful to have Butler's refutation at hand.[2]

In the Preface to his *Sermons*, Butler characterized what we now call psychological egoism as follows:

> There is a strange affectation in many people of explaining away all particular affections, and representing the whole of life as nothing but one continual exercise of self-love. Hence arises that surprising confusion and perplexity in the Epicureans of old, Hobbes, the author [Rochefoucauld] of *Reflections, Sentences, et Maximes Morales*, and this whole set of writers; the confusion of calling actions interested which are done in contradiction to the most manifest known interest, merely for the gratification of a present passion.

This melding of all motives into the single category of self-interest (Butler normally spoke of "self-love") brings about a "total confusion of all language." True, all desires are desires of the self, and in acting to satisfy a desire we seek to satisfy a desire that belongs to the self—"for no one can act but from a desire, or choice, or preference of his own"— but such truisms tell us nothing about the *objectives*, or goals, of our desires, which may be "interested" (self-regarding) or "disinterested." This, as I explained in the previous chapter, became the standard refrain among critics of psychological egoism, but Butler went far beyond this criticism. His *Sermons* contain a fascinating account of the appetites, passions, affections, and propensities in human nature that must be taken into account when considering what constitutes happiness and a good life. Butler also made a significant contribution to the theory of *conscience*—a topic of great interest to 18th-century British Moralists.

Before presenting a summary of Butler's major points, I wish to establish some background. First, we should consider the meanings of "self-love" (or "self-interest") and "selfish." Although Butler usually used "selfish" without any negative connotations, it was not uncommon for British Moralists to distinguish between selfishness and rational self-interest. (Butler used terms like "cool self-love" to describe the latter.)

This passage from Edward Montague's *Reflections on the Rise and Fall of the Ancient Republics Adapted to the Present State of Great Britain* (1759) is quite typical. After affirming "an essential difference between our ideas of self-love and selfishness," Montague continued:

> Self-love, within its due bounds, is the practice of the great duty of self-preservation, regulated by that law which the great Author of our being has given for that very end. Self-love, therefore, is not only compatible with the most rigid practice of the social duties, but is in fact a great motive and incentive to the practice of all moral virtue. Whereas selfishness, by reducing every thing to the single point of private interest, a point which it never loses sight of, banishes all the social virtues.

James Mackintosh drew a similar distinction in *Dissertation on the Progress of Ethical Philosophy*, published in 1830. In his admiring discussion of Butler, Mackintosh wrote:

> A regard to our own general happiness is not a vice, but in itself an excellent quality. It were well if it prevailed more generally over craving and short-sighted appetites. The weakness of the social affections, and

the strength of private desires, properly constitute selfishness; a vice utterly at variance with the happiness of him who harbours it, and, as such, condemned by self-love.

Although Butler, unlike Mackintosh, did not condemn "selfishness" per se as a vice, he did agree with the overall point that Mackintosh was making. Given Butler's attack on psychological egoism, we might expect to find him calling for fewer actions motivated by self-love. But this was not his position; on the contrary, Butler maintained that we need *more* self-love in the world, not less: "The thing to be lamented is, not that men have so great regard to their own good or interest in the present world, for they have not enough." Butler repeatedly pointed to instances of people who sacrifice their authentic self-interest by acting on frivolous impulses and transitory emotions, without considering how those actions will affect their overall happiness. To understand Butler's approach to this problem, we need to understand a few things about his views of human psychology.

According to Butler, if we are to understand human beings and their actions from a *moral* perspective, we must look at human nature as a *system* of interrelated propensities. This system, or "constitution" of human beings, means that we should not view any particular propensity, such as self-interest or benevolence, in isolation from other motives; rather, we need to understand how our motives are related and how they *should* be regulated by reason in order to attain happiness.

Butler identified four basic types of propensities. The first are "particular passions and affections," or motives that cause us to seek or to avoid specific external objectives. The second propensity is "cool self-love," or a reasoned concern for our long-range happiness. The third is benevolence, or a rational concern for the welfare of others. Finally, we have the principle of conscience; this is our power to deliberate rationally over conflicting motives and decide which action will best promote our happiness in the long run.

The most interesting feature of Butler's taxonomy of propensities is his distinction between self-love and particular passions and affections. Self-love, for Butler, is a general principle, a rational power that enables us to evaluate the desirability of specific actions within the context of our long-range happiness. This distinction was also the core of Butler's rejection of psychological egoism. Consider the example of eating food when we are hungry. Many people would call this a self-interested action, but Butler disagreed. We normally eat to satisfy our hunger, not because we assess eating to be in our self-interest. Hunger, not self-interest, is what normally motivates us to eat something. Of course, a consideration of rational self-interest may play a role here, as when we decide that one type of food is better for us than another. Butler freely conceded that real motives are often mixed and difficult to segregate, but he insisted that certain theoretical distinctions should be made if we are truly to understand human action.

Butler applied his analysis of particular propensities to a wide range of actions. For example, when we seek revenge we do so because we want to hurt another person, not because we believe that a particular act of revenge will further our self-interest. On the contrary, vengeful acts may be contrary to our rational self-interest, but we may undertake them anyway without thinking through their long-range consequences. The same general reasoning applies to particular acts of benevolence. If we give money to a panhandler, we do so because we want to help him out, and this motive is not normally accompanied by reflecting on whether our benevolence is consistent with our self-interest. Such considerations come into play only when we rationally reflect on particular actions and types of propensities in order to assess their role, if any, in furthering our own interests, specifically, our long-range happiness.

Butler's analysis leaves a good deal of room for "disinterested" actions—that is, actions that are not motivated by considerations of self-interest. Such actions may or may not be consistent with self-love, but in any case their moral worth does not depend on whether their primary objective is to benefit ourselves or whether we intend to benefit others: "Or, in other words, we may judge and determine, that an action is morally good or evil, before we so much as consider whether it be interested or disinterested." Egoistic actions may be virtuous or vicious, but the same is true of *every* type of action. Even benevolence can be a vice when pushed too far, as when we inflict serious harm on ourselves in an effort to help others. Disinterested actions (those actions undertaken without regard to ourselves) may result in "the utmost possible depravity" of which human nature is capable, as we find in acts of "disinterested cruelty."

Although I had planned to cover Butler's ideas in one chapter, his thinking—especially his claim than many motives are neither self-regarding *or* other-regarding—was so outside the box that I now think it advisable to continue this discussion in the next chapter, in order to clarify some essential points. In addition, I want to discuss some implications of Butler's psychological and moral theories for liberal political thought.

7

Joseph Butler, Continued

In the previous chapter, I explained some basic themes found in Bishop Butler's theory of ethics, much of which includes what we now call psychology. In this chapter, I recap those themes, expand upon them, and summarize Butler's theory of conscience. I strongly recommend that you read the previous chapter before tackling this one.

In regard to our egoistic tendencies that promote our private good, in contrast to those benevolent tendencies that promote the public good, Butler claimed that these ends "do indeed perfectly coincide; and to aim at public and private good are so far from being inconsistent, that they mutually promote each other." (Here as elsewhere we see the influence of Shaftesbury's ideas, discussed in chapter 4, on Butler's thinking.) Butler continued:

> Though benevolence and self-love are different; though the former tends most directly to public good, and the latter to private: yet they are so perfectly coincident, that the greatest satisfactions to ourselves depend upon our having benevolence in a due degree; and . . . self-love is one chief security in our right behavior towards society. It may be added, that their mutual coinciding, so that we can scarce promote one without the other, is equally a proof that we were made for both.

Suppose we were motivated solely by narrow self-interest and never desired to help others. Even here, Butler contended, in an early version of Adam Smith's "invisible hand," that actions based solely on self-interest will often benefit others: "By acting merely from regard (suppose) to reputation, without any consideration of the good of others, men often contribute to the public good." But self-interest is not the only principle that actuates our behavior; we are also motivated by a general principle of benevolence, a disinterested desire to help others. Introspection and experience reveal this other-regarding propensity of human nature with as much certainty as they reveal our self-regarding propensity. That disinterested benevolence motivates many of our actions is evident to common sense, so most people rarely if ever question the existence of the benevolent principle. Only philosophers, said Butler, would deny so obvious a truth, typically by redefining ordinary words in an effort to reduce benevolent actions to disguised forms of self-interest. According to psychological egoists, all actions involve a desire of the self and are efforts to satisfy that desire, so all actions are ultimately self-interested. I discussed Butler's objections to this specious reasoning in the previous chapter; here I will only mention one of his interesting examples. Butler pointed out that the basic argument of psychological egoism would also apply to our reasoning. Suppose we wish to solve a mathematical problem. Well, we desire to solve the problem, and in seeking for a solution we attempt to satisfy that desire. Does this mean that all mathematical reasoning, indeed all reasoning, is self-interested per se? According to Butler, this would be an abuse of language, an absurd way of speaking. But such is the inner logic of psychological egoism.

As I also noted in the previous chapter, Butler denied that every human action is motivated *either* by self-love *or* by benevolence. On the contrary, a vast range of actions results from *particular* desires to attain *concrete* objectives. When we eat because we are hungry, it is hunger, not self-interest, that motivates us to act. When we pity a person in pain and seek to relieve his suffering, it is the desire to lessen his pain, not benevolence, that motivates us to act. As is clear from these examples, some particular impulses are more closely related to self-interest than to benevolence, and vice versa, but it does not follow that the actions stemming from such impulses are motivated by either self-love or benevolence. This is because we frequently act on particular impulses without considering their broader implications. Here is how Butler put it:

> Men have various appetites, passions, and particular affections, quite distinct both from self-love and from benevolence; all of these have a tendency to promote both public and private good, and may be considered as respecting others and ourselves equally and in common; but some of them seem most immediately to respect others, or tend to public good; others of them most immediately to respect self, or tend to private good: as the former are not benevolence, so the latter are not self-love: neither sort are instances of our love either to ourselves or others; but only instances of our Maker's care and love both of the individual and the

species, and proofs that he intended we should be instruments of good to each other, as well as that we should be so to ourselves.

It is only when we rationally examine a specific impulse and place it within the broader context of self-love or benevolence that such actions become either self-interested or benevolent. Thus if I attempt to help a person in pain because I view benevolence (in certain circumstances) as *morally right*, then my action involves more than satisfying a specific desire; now it also entails an attempt to do what I regard as right. The same reasoning applies to particular impulses that may appear self-interested but are not truly so unless they are evaluated as proper means to my happiness. When particular impulses, of whatever type, are not evaluated in this manner, they are apt to be pursued without moderation (or, at the other extreme, insufficiently) and thereby prove detrimental to our happiness. In any case, only when we take an action *because* we believe it will further our own self-interest should that action be classified as self-interested, for only here is our own welfare and happiness the *purpose* of our action.

According to Butler, happiness can be achieved only with the proper balance of our many passions and appetites. Both self-love and benevolence are natural and praiseworthy, and they work in tandem. The benevolent principle restrains our egoistic impulses and tends to hinder us from hurting others in our pursuit of happiness, and the selfish principle likewise restrains our benevolent impulses from being pursued in excess, to the point of harming our essential interests. The proper exercise of both principles is therefore necessary to happiness, and this requires that many particular impulses be subsumed and evaluated within the broader framework of the general principles of self-love and benevolence.

In addition to the features of human nature that I have mentioned so far, Butler included "a principle of reflection in men, by which they distinguish between, approve and disapprove their own actions." This principle of reflection is what Butler called "conscience." This is an extremely important subject in its own right, one that is too often omitted in discussions of the moral theories affiliated with classical liberalism, but here, for the sake of completeness, I will touch upon some basic points. Butler wrote:

> We are plainly constituted such sort of creatures as to reflect upon our own nature. The mind can take a view of what passes within itself, its propensions, aversions, passions, affections, as respecting such objects, and in such degrees; and of the several actions

consequent thereupon. In this survey it approves of one, disapproves of another, and towards a third is affected in neither of these ways, but is quite indifferent. This principle in man, by which he approves or disapproves his heart, temper, and actions, is conscience; for this is the strict sense of the word, though sometimes it is used to take in more. And that this faculty tends to restrain men from doing mischief from each other, and leads them to do good, is too manifest to need being insisted upon.

Butler gave the example of the natural affection that parents feel for their children. This natural impulse typically causes parents to provide basic care for their children, but more is added when parents *deliberately reflect* on their parental obligations. At this point, thanks to the reflective faculty of conscience, "the affection becomes a much more settled principle" and motivates parents to undergo "more labour and difficulties" for the sake of their children than affection alone might bring about. In other words, conscience, after distinguishing between good and bad impulses, transforms our good impulses into matters of *moral principle*—general rules that we ought to follow (and generally do follow) in the absence of extenuating circumstances. Unlike some moral sense theorists, for whom conscience is an innate *feeling*, in effect, Butler viewed conscience as our ability to rationally assess the pros and cons of our particular impulses, rank them according to their importance in the attainment of happiness, and evaluate specific actions accordingly. The categorization of particular passions and affections as either self-regarding or other-regarding is an important part of this process, one that enables the reflective conscience to consider the essential characteristics of actions rather than getting bogged down in nonessential differences.

In a manner similar to Immanuel Kant's later defense of moral autonomy, Butler declared that it is "by this faculty [of conscience], natural to man, that he is a moral agent, that he is a law to himself." We are self-legislating insofar as we must decide for ourselves which moral principles to follow, and in making these decisions conscience has final authority. Unlike Kant, however, Butler did not defend moral duty for its own sake. Rather, Butler regarded happiness as the ultimate end of human action, and happiness cannot be attained by any random means. Like the ancient Stoics, Butler argued that we must follow our nature to achieve happiness; and, well before David Hume called attention to the various meanings of "natural," Butler acknowledged the same ambiguity. As a result, he discussed and excluded several meanings of "nature," after which he explained that in dubbing certain actions "unnatural" he meant actions that are "utterly disproportionate to the nature of man." Happiness requires that the passions and affections that constitute the emotional nature of man must be ordered according to rational principles, as determined by conscience; this is the "natural supremacy, of the faculty which surveys, approves or disapproves the several affections of our mind and actions of our lives, being that by which men are a law to themselves, their conformity or disobedience to which law of our nature renders their actions, in the highest and most proper sense, natural or unnatural."

Butler argued that "natural," morally considered, does not mean acting on a strong impulse or fleeting desire, for such actions will not further the pursuit of happiness, which is natural to man. In no instance should we permit unreasoned desires to trump our rational self-interest.

> If passion prevails over self-love, the consequent action is unnatural; but if self-love prevails over passion, the action is natural: it is manifest that self-love is in human nature a superior principle to passion. If we will act conformably to the economy of man's nature, reasonable self-love must govern.

As with all sketches, my sketch of Butler's theory of moral psychology has omitted a good deal of important material, including some of the arguments he used to defend his ideas. I have devoted considerable space to Butler's ideas for three reasons: first, because of their inherent interest; second, because of their immense influence on subsequent British Moralists, many of whom were classical liberals; and, third, because they illustrate the inextricable connection between psychology and ethics—a connection that was well understood and extensively discussed by classical liberals.

8

Bernard Mandeville

Bernard Mandeville (1670–1733), a Dutch physician who settled in London shortly after earning his degree in medicine at the University of Leyden, is best known as the author of *The Fable of the Bees: or, Private Vices, Publick Benefits* (6th ed., 1729), a work that provoked enormous controversy throughout the 18th century. Mandeville developed a number of important themes—most notably the role of self-interest (so-called vices) in generating a prosperous social order—that would play a crucial role in later libertarian thought. It was largely through the writings of F. A. Hayek, who praised Mandeville as an anti-rationalist and a pioneer in spontaneous order theory, that various libertarian thinkers, especially economists, became interested in him.

Mandeville had good reason to characterize *The Fable of the Bees* as "a rhapsody void of order or method." Written over a period of 24 years, it began as a doggerel poem, "The Grumbling Hive: or, Knaves Turn'd Honest" (1705). In later years (beginning in 1714), Mandeville appended a number of essays, remarks, and dialogues to subsequent editions until what began as a poem of 433 lines came to fill two substantial volumes. This later material—which includes the important theoretical essays "An Enquiry into the Origin of Moral Virtue" and "A Search into the Nature of Society" as well as six dialogues that make up the second volume—are extended commentaries on themes presented in "The Grumbling Hive."

Mandeville's allegory of a beehive extols the social benefits of self-interested actions, such as avarice, greed, and other traditional vices. But it is not always clear what Mandeville meant in claiming that "private vices" produce "public benefits." He depicted the hive as a limited monarchy in which the king's power "was circumsrib'd by Laws"; and in the "Moral" of the poem, Mandeville stated:

So Vice is beneficial found,
When it's by Justice lopt and bound. . . .

This suggests that Mandeville regarded as socially beneficial only those vices that do not violate the rules of justice. This is the interpretation given by F. B. Kaye in the Introduction to his superb edition of the *The Fable of the Bees* (1924):

> Vices are to be punished as soon as they grow into crimes, says Mandeville. . . . The real thesis of the book is not that all evil is a public benefit, but that a certain useful proportion of it (called vice) is such a benefit (and . . . is on that account not really felt to be evil, though still called vicious).

This is a problematic interpretation because Mandeville also discussed the social benefits of unjust actions, such as theft and fraud, which provide employment for those in the criminal justice system, as well as for those artisans and laborers who are needed to replace goods that have been destroyed or stolen. This ambiguity in Mandeville's poem (which appears in his explanatory essays as well) partially accounts for the hostile reception he later received even from those who sympathized with his defense of self-interest. For example, in *The Theory of Moral Sentiments* (1759; 6th ed., 1790), Adam Smith said that Mandeville's arguments "in some respects bordered upon the truth," despite "how destructive this system may appear."

Although Kaye and other commentators have depicted Mandeville as an early proponent of laissez faire, he is more accurately described as a liberal mercantilist, primarily because he argued that government should ensure a favorable balance of trade, and that the lower classes should not be educated above their station, lest they become discontented with menial labor and low wages. He also maintained that private vices could be turned into public benefits only "by the dextrous Management of a skilful Politician." Nevertheless, it is fair to say that Mandeville was sympathetic to some aspects of laissez faire.

One of Mandeville's most influential arguments was his defense of "luxury," which had been widely condemned for its supposedly corrupting effects on social mores. Mandeville's points about the economic benefits of luxury, as well as his criticism of this concept as excessively vague, would later reappear in the writings of David Hume, Edward Gibbon, Adam Smith, and other liberal individualists.

More troublesome was Mandeville's defense of psychological egoism, according to which all actions, even those virtuous actions which appear other-regarding or disinterested, are ultimately motivated by self-interest. It was largely owing to this thesis that Mandeville (like Thomas Hobbes before him) was widely condemned as an enemy of morality. Mandeville responded to this common charge by claiming that he was observing human behavior as it really *is*, not prescribing how it *ought* to be.

Before proceeding with a more detailed account of Mandeville's ideas, I wish to call attention to a serious problem, namely, the conflict between psychological egoism and a theory of spontaneous order rooted in the beneficial effects of self-interested actions (within the boundaries of justice). If psychological egoism is correct, if all actions are ultimately motivated by self-interest, then to argue for the benefits of self-interested actions in developing and maintaining social order tells us virtually nothing. For, if *all* actions are self-interested, if nonegoistic actions are *impossible*, then we have no point of contrast by which we can distinguish some kinds of motives from others. And in this case *any* action may be said to promote social order. Even social planners would be acting from self-interest, according to psychological egoism, so even their actions could be praised as conducive to social order. Only in a thinker like Adam Smith, who distinguished self-interest from beneficence, does the appeal to an "invisible hand" make sense, for only if we contrast self-interested actions with other kinds of actions is it possible to isolate the former and explore the social benefits of self-interest, in contrast to other kinds of motives. For a psychological egoist like Mandeville, however, no such contrast is possible, so it becomes meaningless to praise self-interested actions for their social benefits because this would entail nothing more than praising *all* human actions, without distinction, for their social benefits.

Adam Ferguson and other critics of psychological egoism were therefore correct: if, through a linguistic coup, we collapse all kinds of actions into the category of self-interest, then we will need to invent a new and needless vocabulary that enables us to distinguish between different types of motives within the generic category of self-interested actions. Only in this way would we be able to explain and defend the traditional theory of spontaneous order. (See chapter 5 for Ferguson's objections to "the selfish system.") Despite this fatal flaw in Mandeville's approach, he had many worthwhile and provocative things to say, especially about conventional notions of vice; and these ideas may be abstracted from his fundamental principles and evaluated on their own merits.

Now let's take a brief look at the historical context in which Mandeville offered his ideas about the beneficial effects of vice.

When Mandeville moved to England during the 1690s (while he was in his 20s), he encountered a widespread movement to suppress personal vices. The Glorious Revolution of 1688 was widely viewed by pious Christians not only as a revolution for the rights of Englishmen but also as a revolution against moral corruption. The Stuart kings, it was said, had tolerated and even encouraged immorality (drunkenness, whoring, etc.) among their subjects as a means of maintaining political control; only a virtuous citizenry will resist tyranny. On April 4, 1699, the Archbishop of Canterbury issued a Circular Letter in which he called for the suppression of vice and encouraged pious Christians to report offenders to magistrates:

> Every pious Person of the Laity should, if need be, be put in Mind, that he ought to think himself obliged to use his best Endeavours to have such Offenders punished by the Civil Magistrates, as can be no otherwise amended; and that when he hears his Neighbour Swear, or Blaspheme the Name of God, or sees him offend in Drunkenness or Prophanation of the Lord's-Day, he ought to give the Magistrate Notice of it. In such a Case to be called an Informer, will be so far from making any Man odious in the Judgment of sober Persons, that it will tend to his Honour, when he makes it appear by his unblameable Behaviour,

and that Care that he takes of himself and his Family, that he doth it purely for the Glory of God, and the Good of his Brethren. Such well-disposed Persons as are resolved upon this, should be encouraged to meet as often as they can, to consult how they may most discreetly and effectually manage it in the Place where they live.

On February 20, 1702, Queen Anne, just one month after ascending the throne, issued *A Proclamation for the Encouragement of Piety and Virtue, and for the Preventing and Punishing of Prophaneness and Immorality.* The Queen complained that the laws against vice were not being adequately enforced, and she wanted that changed:

It is an indispensable Duty on Us, to be careful, above all other things, to preserve and advance the Honour and Service of Almighty God, and to discourage and suppress all Vice, Prophaneness, Debauchery, and Immorality, which are so highly displeasing to God, so great a Reproach to Our Religion and Government, and (by means of the frequent ill Examples of the Practicers thereof) have so fatal a Tendency to the Corruption of many of Our Loving Subjects, otherwise Religiously and Virtuously disposed, and which (if not timely remedied) may justly draw down the Divine Vengeance on Us and Our Kingdoms. . . . To the Intent, therefore, that Religion, Piety, and good Manners may (according to Our most hearty Desire) flourish and increase under our Administration and Government, We have thought fit (by the Advice of Our Privy Council) to issue this Our Royal Proclamation, and do hereby declare our Royal Purpose and Resolution to discountenance and punish all manner of *Vice*, *Prophaneness*, and *Immorality*, in all Persons of whatever Degree or Quality, within this Our Realm.

Here we see one of the most common early arguments for vice laws. Because God (as illustrated in the Bible, especially the Old Testament) inflicts collective vengeance, punishing the many for the sins of the few, rulers must suppress and punish supposedly private vices as a means of protecting society as a whole from the divine wrath of plagues, famines, military defeats, and so forth. Incidentally, this was one reason why Enlightenment libertarians stressed the importance of science, which teaches that such disasters result from *natural* causes. Individual freedom, these early libertarians believed, cannot gain a solid foothold in a world where the innocent are punished along with the guilty because there exists no room in this scheme for the argument that private vices harm *only* the individuals who practice them. (A secular version of this argument has survived to this day among defenders of vice laws, but I must leave this interesting controversy for a later book.)

In 1701, England had about 20 "Societies for the Reformation of Manners." (In that day, "manners" meant what we now call "morality" or "morals.") These societies relied heavily on informers to hunt down sinners. As Thomas A. Horne explained in *The Social Thought of Bernard Mandeville: Virtue and Commerce in Early Eighteenth Century England* (1978):

> The English legal system in this period relied upon information given by private individuals and this procedure made it possible for a group like the Societies for the Reformation of Manners to become actively involved in law enforcement. According to a student of this period, "a private person could obtain a warrant from a Justice of the Peace or Magistrate, sometimes on his unsupported evidence, and this warrant

of conviction the constable of the parish was required to execute." After the convicted persons paid a fine or served a term in jail they could sue for false charges, but if they lost they had to pay treble costs. The societies, with the help of friendly magistrates, distributed blank warrants to its members, who filled in the names of wrongdoers, and collected the filled-in warrants to return them to the magistrates.

. . . It appears . . . that the members of the society were rarely informers themselves, but employed others to inform for a fee. The practice of informing was no more popular then than it is now, and the informers soon became the symbols of the societies to their enemies.

Given the moral fanaticism that prevailed when Mandeville took up residence in London, we can appreciate why his argument that private vices may produce unintended public benefits evoked furious denunciations not only against Mandeville's ideas but also against him personally. "*The Fable of the Bees*," according to Kaye, "made a public scandal," and it would "be difficult to overrate the intensity and extent of Mandeville's 18th-century fame."

In the next chapter, I take a closer look at some of the ideas that made Mandeville so notorious.

9

Mandeville on the Benefits of Vice

Before continuing my discussion of Bernard Mandeville, I wish to call attention to one of his most astute critics: the Scotch-Irish philosopher Francis Hutcheson (1694–1746), who was Adam Smith's teacher at the University of Glasgow. In his oration "On the Natural Sociability of Mankind" (1730), Hutcheson expanded upon one of his many objections to Mandeville's ideas. According to Mandeville, the desire to socialize with others (beyond the family unit) is not innate in human nature. Rather, societies first came into existence because of the threat posed by wild animals; families allied with other families in order to protect themselves from this danger. And *civilized* societies did not form until *written* laws enforced by government made their appearance. Before then contracts could not be enforced, so life was necessarily insecure and hazardous in that anarchistic "state of nature." In this respect Mandeville was a disciple of Thomas Hobbes; in both we find utter disregard for customs and social conventions, or so-called *unwritten* law. As Mandeville put it:

> It is inconsistent with the Nature of human Creatures, that any Number of them should ever live together in tolerable Concord, without [written] Laws and Government, let the soil, the Climate, and their Plenty be whatever the most luxuriant Imagination should be please'd to fancy them.

Ironically, given F. A. Hayek's praise for Mandeville's treatment of spontaneous order, Francis Hutcheson criticized Mandeville for his "constructivism"—Hayek's label for the erroneous belief that societies and major institutions were consciously constructed, or designed. Hutcheson, contrary to Mandeville, maintained that societies did not originate from deliberate calculations of self-interest, such as the perceived utility of mutual security from external dangers. Rather, early societies were formed "without any art of deliberation, indeed without any previous command of the will," even when there was "no prospect of private advantage." This is far more Hayekian than Mandeville's theory (which he discussed at length in the second volume of *The Fable of the Bees*) that societies originated in estimates of personal utility, specifically, from the desire to mitigate the dangers posed by wolves, lions, boars, bears, and so forth.

Because I will be discussing Hutcheson in the next chapter, I will not pursue his objections to Mandeville in more detail for now. I mention this subject because Hayek's ideas about the early history of classical liberalism, which have influenced many libertarian scholars, are misleading in some respects, and sometimes seriously so. The doctrine of natural rights, as defended by Hutcheson and the natural-law school of liberalism generally (but not by Mandeville), was "rationalistic" in Hayek's pejorative sense of the term. Yet, when we take a close look at those ideas, we will sometimes find them more congenial to Hayek's social and political philosophy than what we find in the writings of Mandeville and other "anti-rationalists." Hayek exacerbated the problem when he differentiated between the "French" (rationalist) and "English" (anti-rationalist) schools of classical liberalism—a Burkean distinction (later developed more fully by the political theorist Francis Lieber in his 1849 article, "Anglican and Gallican

Liberty") with little foundation in the history of classical liberalism. Hayek's dichotomy was rendered plausible only by his selective cherry-picking of representatives for each school. His line of demarcation is so porous and indistinct as to be virtually useless in our effort to understand the intellectual history of classical liberalism and the major disagreements among liberals.

Now, having satisfied my editorial proclivities, let's begin our examination of some of Mandeville's fundamental ideas by taking a brief look at his celebrated rhymed allegory, "The Grumbling Hive: or, Knaves Turn'd Honest," which was originally published anonymously in 1705. Mandeville later said of this piece:

> I do not dignify these few loose lines with the Name of a Poem, that I would have the Reader expect any poetry in them, but barely because they are Rhime, and I am in reality puzzled by what Name to give them. . . . All I can say of them is, that they are a Story told in Dogrel, which without the least design of being Witty, I have endeavour'd to do in as easy and familiar a manner as I was able: The Reader shall be welcome to call them what he pleases.

The poem begins:

> A Spacious Hive well stockt with Bees,
> That liv'd in Luxury and Ease;
> And yet as fam'd for Laws and Arms,
> As yielding large and early Swarms;
> Was counted the great Nursery
> Of Sciences and Industry.

Mandeville explained how the prosperity of this hive was made possible by the widespread practice of traditional vices.

> Vast Numbers throng'd the fruitful Hive;
> Yet those vast Numbers made 'em thrive;
> Millions endeavouring to supply
> Each other's Lust and Vanity. . . .

The popular vices in the hive included fraud and theft.

> Pick-pockets, Coiners, Quacks, South-sayers,
> And all those, that in Enmity,
> With downright Working, cunningly
> Convert to their own Use the Labour
> Of their good-natur'd heedless Neighbour.
> These were call'd Knaves, but bar the Name,
> The grave Industrious were the same. . . .

Here we see a problem that I mentioned in the previous chapter—namely, that Mandeville did not restrict his discussion of the unintended social benefits generated by self-interested actions within the boundaries of justice; he applied the same reasoning to various crimes. And this is what largely precipitated the hostile criticisms later voiced by those classical liberals, such as Adam Smith, who agreed that self-interested actions generate social benefits that were not intended by the acting agent (Smith's "invisible hand"), but who refused to include unjust, or rights-violating, actions in the category of socially beneficial actions.

Indeed, elsewhere Mandeville argued for the economic benefits of shipwrecks, which create employment for those workers needed to replace lost vessels. He also claimed that similar benefits flow from major disasters, such as the Great London Fire of 1666, which gutted the city and left about 70,000 people without homes. It is scarcely possible to conceive of more stark examples of what Frédéric Bastiat called the "broken window fallacy," a type of faulty economic reasoning that ignores opportunity costs. The labor and capital needed to replace lost ships and buildings merely restore the status quo; and if not for such disasters those resources would have been used to satisfy other economic opportunities that had to be sacrificed to replace what had been destroyed. An especially frustrating element in Mandeville's economic reasoning, as a number of his critics were quick to point out, is that it shows no understanding of opportunity costs.

This is not to say that Mandeville failed to distinguish personal vices from crimes; he did make that distinction; but, lacking a theory of rights, he was vague on how and where the line should be drawn between the two categories. Instead, he repeatedly said that dexterous and skillful politicians should manage the problem by regulating vices so that they do not create more harm than good. We find this argument in his 1724 tract, *A Modest Defence of Publick Stews: or, An Essay Upon Whoring*, which calls for legalized but regulated prostitution. This vice, whether legal or illegal, will always be widespread "as long as it is the Nature of Man . . . to have a Salt Itch in the Breeches [and] the Brimstone under the Petticoat." Laws against prostitution do little if anything to curb the practice; they merely drive underground the problems associated with this vice. "What avails it then to affect to conceal that which cannot be concealed, and that which if carried on openly and above-board would become only less detrimental, and of consequence more justifiable?"

The same line of reasoning is also found in *The Fable of the Bees: or, Private Vices, Publick Benefits.* "The Passions of some

People," Mandeville wrote, "are too violent to be curb'd by any Law or Precept; and it is Wisdom in all Governments to bear with lesser Inconveniences to prevent greater." Legal prostitution, if wisely regulated by government, will yield better results than illegal prostitution. In a manner surprisingly similar to the defense of legal prostitution given many centuries earlier by the sainted Catholic theologian Thomas Aquinas (in *Summa Theologica*), Mandeville defended his position as follows:

> If Courtezans and Strumpets were to be prosecuted with as much Rigor as some Silly People would have it, what Locks or Bars would be sufficient to preserve the Honour of our Wives and Daughters? For 'tis not only that the Women in general would meet with far greater Temptations, and the Attempts to ensnare the Innocence of Virgins would seem more excusable even to the sober part of Mankind than they do now: But some men would grow outrageous, and Ravishing would become a common Crime. Where six or seven Thousand Sailors arrive at once, as it often happens at *Amsterdam* [Mandeville, remember, was Dutch], that have seen none but their own sex for many Months together, how is it to be suppos'd that

honest Women should walk the streets unmolested, if there were no Harlots to be had at reasonable prices? For which Reason the Wise Rulers of that well-or-der'd City always tolerate an uncertain number of Houses, in which Women are hired as publickly as Horses at a Livery-Stable.

As we see here, Mandeville appealed to the social utility of vices, as determined in specific cases by politicians, as the determining factor when deciding whether particular vices should be legal or illegal. Individual rights, such as the right of a woman to use her own body as she sees fit, played no role in Mandeville's reasoning. Thus in explaining the benefits of various vices, Mandeville meant that their *social consequences* are beneficial as a whole, regardless of the motives behind immoral actions or how such actions may harm the person who engages in them. This naturally raises the key question of what Mandeville himself meant by "virtue" and "vice," which I address in the next chapter. I conclude this chapter by explaining the conclusion reached by Mandeville in "The Grumbling Hive."

In a send-up of the Societies for the Reformation of Manners (discussed in the previous chapter), Mandeville considered what would happen if some pious, moralistic bees succeeded in eradicating all vices from their hive. After Jove granted their wish, the result was a society without prosperity.

> THEN leave Complaints: Fools only strive
> To make a Great an Honest Hive.
> T' enjoy the World's Conveniencies,
> Be fam'd in War, yet live in Ease,
> Without great Vices, is a vain
> Eutopia seated in the Brain.
> Fraud, Luxury and Pride must live,
> While we the Benefits receive. . . .
> So Vice is beneficial found,
> When it's by Justice lopt and bound;
> Nay, where the People would be great,
> As necessary to the State,
> As Hunger is to make 'em eat.
> Bare Virtue can't make Nations live
> In Spendour; they, that would revive
> A Golden Age.
> Must be as free,
> For Acorns, as for Honesty.

10

Bernard Mandeville vs. Francis Hutcheson

It might be helpful to summarize a basic controversy concerning the natural sociability of humankind. In other words, is the desire of people to interact with other people (beyond the family unit) and to form enduring associations called "society" a natural propensity of human beings? Or do people form societies only *after* utilitarian calculations reveal that such associations will advance the self-interested goals of the participants?

Those many classical liberals who upheld the natural sociability of man did not deny that self-interested considerations played a role in the early history of societies; but they also maintained that humans have a natural propensity—or *instinct*, as it was sometimes called—to interact with other humans, and that the benefits accruing from this interaction were not foreseen or designed by the participants. Explicit calculations of personal utility occurred only *after* societies had been formed, for only then were people able to experience the benefits of social life and subsequently strive to maintain the conditions, such as justice, that made those benefits possible.

As I explained in previous chapters, Thomas Hobbes and Bernard Mandeville were two of the most influential philosophers who denied the natural sociability of man—and, not coincidentally, both were psychological egoists who argued that all human actions are ultimately motivated by self-interested considerations. Consequently, if all actions are driven by self-interested desires, people would never have formed societies unless they believed, *prior* to their entry into a society, that such interaction would benefit them personally. For Hobbes, our egoistic proclivities in a state of nature (a society without government) would result in a perpetual war of every man against every man, so a stable social order was not possible until an absolute government instilled the fear of death in its subjects, after which this self-interested fear trumped our violent, predatory instincts to harm or kill others in the course of getting what we want.

Mandeville agreed with Hobbes in some respects, but he added his own twist. He did not believe that threats of violence by a government would have resulted in social order, but he did believe that people needed "the curb of government" to sustain a peaceful, productive society. In a theory that smacks of Hayekian constructivism (a notion that I explained in the previous chapter), Mandeville speculated that governments appealed to the vanity and pride of people rather than to their fears. Rulers (and other "wise men" in league with government) subdued the natural bent of humans to please themselves by convincing them "that it was more beneficial for every Body to conquer than indulge his Appetites, and much better to mind the Publick than what seem'd his private interest." In pursuit of this objective, wise rulers were unable to provide any "real rewards" that would compensate for the sacrifice of egoistic pursuits for the public good, so they examined "all the Strength and Frailties of our Nature"; and they concluded that "Flattery must be the most powerful Argument that could be used" to divert people from their narrow self-interested pursuits in favor of the public good. It was by using the "bewitching Engine" of flattery that rulers appealed to the natural vanity of human beings by persuading them that they were rational creatures

"capable of performing the most noble Achievements."
Mandeville continued:

> Having by this artful way of Flattery insinuated
> themselves into the Hearts of Men, [rulers] began to
> instruct them in the Notions of Honour and Shame;
> representing [Shame] as the worst of all Evils, and
> the other as the highest Good to which Mortals could
> aspire: Which being done, they laid before them how
> unbecoming it was the Dignity of such sublime Crea-
> tures to be solicitous about gratifying those Appe-
> tites, which they had in common with Brutes, and
> at the same time unmindful of those higher Quali-
> ties that gave them the preeminence over all visible
> Beings. They indeed confess'd, that those impulses
> of Nature were very pressing; that it was troublesome
> to resist, and very difficult wholly to subdue them.
> But this they only used as an Argument to demon-
> strate, how glorious the Conquest of them was on the
> one hand, and how scandalous on the other not to
> attempt it.

As illustrated in these remarks, Mandeville substituted
vanity and pride for Hobbesian fear in his explanation of how
self-interest can be manipulated by government so as to make

social order possible. Pride, like fear, is an egoistic motive, so both schemes never waver from the thesis that self-interest alone drives human actions. But whereas the Hobbesian fear of death is quite real, pride, as explained by Mandeville, is a type of deception inculcated by rulers and their philosophical allies. Individuals who believe themselves to be noble, altruistic, or public-spirited are deceiving themselves; such individuals are in fact motivated by the desire to be praised and flattered by others—the wellsprings of egoistic pride.

Although Mandeville discussed and defended his thesis in detail throughout both volumes of *The Fable of the Bees: or, Private Vices, Publick Benefits*, it would serve no purpose to follow him further. It should be noted, however, that this aspect of Mandeville's social theory does not harmonize with his reputation as a pioneer in the theory of spontaneous order and social evolution. It may be true, as F. B. Kaye (editor of the definitive edition of *The Fable of the Bees*) maintained, that Mandeville did not mean to say that wise rulers perpetrated their psychological manipulation at one time in order to kick-start social order but that, instead, the process occurred over a long period. This qualification was necessary if Kaye was to defend his claim that Mandeville was a pioneer in historical sociology and anthropology—a claim echoed by F. A. Hayek and other scholars, including libertarian scholars. A problem here is that Mandeville reveled in positing paradoxes, with the result that he sometimes seemed to defend inconsistent positions. But the passages I quoted are from "An Enquiry Into the Origin of Moral Virtue" (in the first volume of *The Fable of the Bees*), which is one of Mandeville's most important pieces. And there we find an implausible—indeed, fanciful—theory that treats social order as a construction, in effect, of wise rulers who manipulated their subjects psychologically as a means to further the public good. How rulers became so much wiser than their subjects, Mandeville did not attempt to explain. (His approach reminds me of those skeptics of ancient Greece who argued that rulers deliberately concocted the gods as a means of maintaining political control.)

Mandeville's theory of the origin of moral virtue—pride begot by flattery—brings us to his conceptions of "virtue" and "vice." According to Mandeville, whether an action is morally good (a virtue) or morally bad (a vice) depends entirely on the *motives* that actuated it. Good actions are motivated solely by a concern for others, whereas morally bad actions are motivated by self-interest. In this theory of "moral rigorism" (as Kaye called it), no action can be morally good if it is motivated by self-interest, and it was by using this conception of vice that Mandeville defended his celebrated thesis that private vices generate public benefits. When boiled down to essentials, this is to say nothing more than that self-interested actions frequently benefit society as a whole. This was scarcely news to the many moral philosophers, both before and after Mandeville, who had no objections to the pursuit of self-interest, rightly understood. Mandeville's scandalous pronouncement rested almost entirely on his substitution of "vice" for "self-interest."

In *Remarks Upon The Fable of the Bees* (1750), Francis Hutcheson (whom I mentioned in the previous chapter) noted the ambiguity in Mandeville's claim that private vices produce public benefits, a proposition that may be understood in five different ways. But Mandeville, according to Hutcheson, never explained precisely what he meant. If all he meant to say was that self-interested actions sometimes produce social benefits, then Mandeville scored an easy victory by defining "virtue" too narrowly. Self-interested actions are not necessarily immoral, and self-love is quite compatible with benevolence. As Hutcheson put it in *On the Natural Sociability of Mankind* (1730), "the innate self-love of our nature [is] in no way contrary to our common and benevolent affections."

In *Remarks*, Hutcheson also attacked Mandeville for his arbitrary definitions of certain vices. Contrary to Mandeville, for example, the vice of "luxury" did not refer to the enjoyment of goods that are not absolutely necessary for our survival;

rather, the vice of "luxury" signified purchasing goods that one cannot reasonably afford—at the expense of one's obligation to care for one's family. Similarly, for Mandeville the vice of "pride" did not condemn legitimate accomplishments that deserved the esteem and praise of others; rather, it meant "having an opinion for our own virtues . . . greater than what they really are; arrogating to ourselves either obedience, service, or external marks of honour to which we have no right." And "intemperance" did not mean the effort to satisfy any sensual desire; rather, to Mandeville, it referred to "that use of meat and drink which is pernicious to the health and vigour of any person in the discharge of the offices of life."

These vices, Hutcheson went on to explain, will vary according to the characteristics and situations of individuals. "Every one's own knowledge, and experience of his constitution and fortune, will suggest to him what is suitable to his own circumstances." Mandeville's claim "that using any thing above the bare necessaries of life is intemperance, pride, or luxury" is, according to Hutcheson, simply "ridiculous." It is not as if "temperance, frugality, or moderation, denoted fixed weights or measures or sums, which all were to observe, and not a proportion to men's circumstances." In short, many vices as defined by Mandeville are not true vices at all, but are merely the reasonable pursuit of self-interest.

Adam Smith later expressed similar objections in *The Theory of Moral Sentiments* (1759; 6th ed., 1790). Mandeville's approach is "wholly pernicious" because it "seems to take away altogether the distinction between vice and virtue." Mandeville was wrong to equate self-interest with vice, "since self-love may frequently be a virtuous motive of action." Moreover, contrary to Mandeville, Smith maintained, "the desire of doing what is honourable and noble, of rendering ourselves the proper objects of esteem and approbation, cannot with any propriety be called vanity. Even the love of well-grounded fame and reputation, the desire of acquiring esteem by what is really estimable, does not deserve that name."

In the final analysis, therefore, neither Hutcheson nor Smith disagreed with Mandeville about the socially beneficial effects of self-interested actions (if pursued within the boundaries of justice). Their major objection was that Mandeville created his paradox of private vices and public benefits by defining "vice" so arbitrarily and narrowly as to tarnish *all* self-interested actions as types of vice.

But what of Mandeville's argument that authentic vices (e.g., theft) and even natural disasters (e.g., shipwrecks) generate socially beneficial outcomes because of the employment they create? Hutcheson (in *Remarks*) replied by invoking opportunity costs (a topic I discussed in the previous chapter).

Consider the drunkard who neglects his family to buy liquor, or the dandy who buys expensive clothes that he cannot reasonably afford. According to Mandeville, such excesses benefit society because someone must produce the liquor and clothes needed to satisfy those vices. But, as Hutcheson pointed out, if the drunkard had spent his money on food and clothes for his family instead of on liquor, that alternative would also have created employment. The same reasoning applies to the dandy and his expensive clothes, as well as to shipwrecks and other examples discussed by Mandeville. It is consumer demand, not vices per se, that keeps the wheels of commerce turning. To attribute the benefits of commerce to private vices was merely a perverse and misleading way of saying the same thing.

Notes

[1] George H. Smith, "Self-Interest and Social Order in Classical Liberalism: Shaftesbury," 2014, Libertarianism.org, October 17, 2014.

[2] C. D. Broad, *Five Types of Ethical Theory* (London: Routledge, 1930), p. 55.

Index

absolutism, 38, 42, 45–49, 104

Analogy of Religion (Butler), 62

"Anglican and Gallican Liberty" (Lieber), 95–96

Anne, Queen, 88–89

Aquinas, Thomas, 100

Areopagitica (Milton), 6, 11

Aristotle, 5

autonomy, moral, 9, 78

Bastiat, Frédéric, 98

benevolence
 in Butler, 62, 67, 68, 72, 74–76
 in Ferguson, 55–56
 in Hobbes, 39
 in human nature, 10, 72–73
 in Hume, 58, 60
 in Hutcheson, 109
 justice and, 27
 restraint of, 76
 self-interest and, 10, 32, 57–58, 68, 74
 in Smith, 7–8
 social order and, 42, 54
 as vice, 69

Bentham, Jeremy, 17

Bible, 89

Branden, Nathaniel, 51–52, 54

British Moralism, 32, 53–54, 60, 64, 80

Broad, C. D., 63

"broken window fallacy," 98

Buckle, Stephen, 18

Butler, Joseph, 54, 60, 61–69,
71–80

Cato's Letters (Trenchard and
Gordon), 48

children, 26–27, 77

Clarke, Samuel, 21, 22–23, 61

conscience, 64, 67, 76–79

constructivism, 94, 105

Cooper, Anthony Ashley, 20, 37

covenant. See social contract

De Cive (Hobbes), 39, 40–41

De Homine (Hobbes), 39

Discourse upon Natural Religion
(Clarke), 21

disinterested actions, 27, 38,
57–60, 69, 72–73

Dissertation on the Progress
of Ethical Philosophy
(Mackintosh), 65–66

division of labor, 25

egoism, psychological, 37–39,
53–54, 57–58, 62–63,
84–85. See also self-interest

Enlightenment, 89–90

Enquiries Concerning Human
Understanding and
Concerning the Principles of
Morals (Hume), 15

Enquiry Concerning the
Principles of Morals, An
(Hume), 15, 56–57

Essay Concerning Human
Understanding, An (Locke),
14–15

Essay on the History of Civil
Society, An (Ferguson),
54–55

ethics. See also British
Moralism; entries at moral

in Branden, 52

in Butler, 71

in Hume, 16, 18

moral rationalism and, 21

political philosophy and, 8–9

theory of knowledge and, 15

Fable of the Bees: or, Private Vices, Publick Benefits (Mandeville), 81–82, 91, 95, 99–100, 107

family, 25–29, 77, 93, 103, 110

fear
  in British Moralism, 53–54
  government and, 41–42, 46, 52–53, 104
  in Hobbes, 42–43, 48, 58
  justice and, 52–53
  pride vs., 106–7
  as restraint, 9, 41, 54
  self-interest and, 41–43, 104
  social contract and, 46, 48
  social order and, 9, 41–42, 49, 104

Ferguson, Adam, 54–56, 86

Fifteen Sermons on Human Nature (Butler), 62, 63

flattery, 105–6, 107, 108

For the New Intellectual: The Philosophy of Ayn Rand (Rand), 13–14

Gert, Bernard, 39

Gibbon, Edward, 84

Glorious Revolution, 87–88

God, 87–89

Gordon, Thomas, 48

government
  absolute, 38, 42, 46–49, 104
  fear and, 41–42, 46, 52–53, 104
  flattery and, 105–6
  in history of term "political," 5, 6
  in Hobbes, 38, 42, 46–48
  justice and, 6, 9–10
  in Mandeville, 83–84, 94, 100, 105
  self-interest and, 106–7
  social contract and, 46
  virtue promotion by, 9–10

"Grumbling Hive: or, Knaves Turn'd Honest" (Mandeville), 82, 96–98, 101

happiness, 5, 65–68, 75–76, 78–79

Hayek, F. A., 17, 81, 94–96, 105, 107

hedonism, psychological, 38

Hendel, Charles W., 15

Hobbes, Thomas, 10, 37–49, 52–53, 58–59, 94, 104–7

Horne, Thomas A., 90–91

human nature
  benevolence in, 10, 72–73
  in British Moralism, 53
  in Butler, 64, 66–67, 72–76, 78–79
  cooperation and, 44
  in Ferguson, 55
  in Hobbes, 40–41
  in Hume, 32, 33, 34, 58
  in Mandeville, 93
  political philosophy and, 1–2

Hume, David, 13–29, 53, 56–60, 62, 78, 84

Hutcheson, Francis, 93–95, 109–12

"Isn't Everyone Selfish?" (Branden), 51

justice
  absolute government and, 47–48
  as artificial, 18–19
  benevolence and, 27
  favoritism and, 27, 28–29
  fear and, 52–53
  government and, 6, 9–10
  in Hobbes, 46
  in Hume, 18–19, 29–30, 34–35
  in libertarianism, 7–9
  in Mandeville, 82–83, 85, 98
  natural law and, 19
  political philosophy and, 2–3
  property and, 31–33
  reason and, 19–20, 34–35
  self-interest and, 103–4
  in Smith, 7–8
  as social concept, 2, 19–20
  social order and, 3, 19–20, 35
  vice and, 82–83

Kant, Immanuel, 78

Kaye, F. B., 83, 91, 107, 108

knowledge. *See also* truth
  in Hume, 14–15
  logical demonstration of, 21
  in Milton, 11
  in Rand, 13–14

labor
  "broken window fallacy"
    and, 98
  division of, 25
  society and, 26
laissez faire, 83–84
La Rochefoucauld. *See*
  Rochefoucauld
Law of Nature, in Hobbes,
  44–45. *See also* natural
  law
"Legal and Political Philosophy of David Hume, The"
  (Hayek), 17
Leviathan (Hobbes), 38,
  42–43
libertarianism
  Enlightenment, 89–90
  justice in, 7–9

Lieber, Francis, 95–96
Life of David Hume, The
  (Mossner), 62
Locke, John, 14–15
luxury, 84, 109–10

Mackintosh, James, 65–66
Mandeville, Bernard, 81–91,
  93–112
material possessions, 27–29
Milton, John, 6, 10–11
*Modest Defence of Publick Stews:
  or, An Essay Upon Whoring*
  (Mandeville), 99
Montague, Edward, 65
moral autonomy, 9, 78
moral corruption, 87. *See also*
  vice
moral distinctions, 15
moral psychology, 79–80
moral rationalism, 20–23
moral rigorism, 108
moral subjectivism, 18
Mossner, Ernest Campbell,
  62

natural law
  in Hume, 18
  justice and, 19
  as rationalistic, 95
*Natural Law and the Theory of
    Property: Grotius to Hume*
    (Buckle), 18
nature, state of, 34, 41, 44–48,
    53, 104
normative political philosophy,
    1–2

objectives
  in Butler, 69, 73
  in motivation, 64, 73–74
  self-love and, 69
Objectivist Newsletter, The
    (Rand), 51
"Of Self-Love" (Hume), 56–57
Old Testament, 89
opportunity cost, 98–99, 111
order. *See* social order

pity, 58, 74
Plato, 5

political, meaning of term, 5–6
positive political philosophy, 1–2
pride, 105–8, 110
private good, 71–72
*Proclamation for the Encourage-
    ment of Piety and Virtue,
    and for the Preventing and
    Punishing of Prophaneness
    and Immorality,* 88–89
propensities
  in Butler, 64, 66–68
  self-interest and, 72–73
property
  in Hume, 27–29, 29–31
  justice and, 31–32, 31–33
  security and, 29–30, 31
  self-interest and, 31–34
  society and, 29–31
prostitution, 99–101
psychological egoism, 37–39,
    53–54, 57–58, 62–63,
    84–85. *See also* self-interest
psychological hedonism, 38
public good, 71–72, 74, 105, 108
Pufendorf, Samuel, 48

Queen Anne, 88–89

Rand, Ayn, 13–14, 15
rationalism
  in Hayek, 95–96
  moral, 20–21, 22–23, 35
reason
  cooperation and, 26
  in Hume, 16, 19, 32
  justice and, 19–20, 34–35
  moral rationalism and,
    20–21
  self-interest and, 32
reflection, 18–19, 33, 57, 76
Reflections, Sentences, et
    Maximes Morales
    (Rochefoucauld), 63
Reflections on the Rise and Fall
    of the Ancient Republics
    Adapted to the Present
    State of Great Britain
    (Montague), 65
Remarks Upon The Fable of the
    Bees (Hutcheson), 109–10
Rochefoucauld, 63

science, 3, 89–90
Second Defence of the English
    People, The (Milton), 10
security
  property and, 29–30, 31
  society and, 26
self-interest
  benevolence and, 10, 32,
    57–58, 68, 74
  in Branden, 51–52, 54
  in Butler, 62–66, 71–73, 79
  disinterested actions and,
    69
  fear and, 41–43, 104
  in Ferguson, 54–56
  government and, 106–7
  in Hobbes, 38–39
  in Hume, 56–57, 58–59
  interest vs., 54–55
  justice and, 103–4
  in Mackintosh, 65–66
  in Mandeville, 82–83,
    84–85, 108–9
  pity and, 58
  property and, 31–34

and psychological egoism,
    37–39, 57–58
  in Smith, 10
  social benefits of, 85–86
  as sole motivator, 10
  vice and, 110
self-love, 57, 62–68, 72–76, 79
sentimentalism, 20, 23
Smith, Adam, 7–10, 23, 83–85,
    93, 98, 111
social contract, 45–48
social order
  absolute government and, 38,
    49, 104–5
  as construction, 108
  fear and, 9, 42, 49, 104
  in Hobbes, 44–45, 53, 104
  justice and, 3, 19–20, 35
  political philosophy and, 1, 2
  self-interest and, 10, 85,
    106–7
  vice and, 81
Social Thought of Bernard
    Mandeville, The: Virtue
    and Commerce in Early

Eighteenth Century England
    (Horne), 90–91
Societies for the Reformation
    of Manners, 90–91, 101–2
society
  as advantageous to man,
    25–27
  benefits to, of self-interested
    actions, 85–86
  children and, 26–27
  in Hutcheson, 94–95
  in Mandeville, 93–94
  property and, 29–31
specialization, 25
state of nature, 34, 41, 44–48,
    53, 104
subjectivism, 18
sufficiency, in political
    philosophy, 3, 4–5
Summa Theologica (Aquinas),
    100

Theory of Moral Sentiments, The
    (Smith), 7, 10, 83, 111
Tönnies, Ferdinand, 48

Treatise of Human Nature, A
(Hume), 16, 18–19
Trenchard, John, 48
truth. *See also* knowledge
demonstrated, 21–22
eternal, 19

utopian society, 5

vanity, 40–41, 105–6, 111
vice
benefits of, 93–102
benevolence as, 69
crime vs., 99
Glorious Revolution and,
87–88

in Hutcheson, 109–10
justice and, 82–83
laws, 9–10, 89, 90
in Mackintosh, 65–66
in Mandeville, 82–83,
97–102, 108–12
in Milton, 11
moral rationalism and, 20–21
Queen Anne and, 88–89
self-interest and, 110
social order and, 81
and Societies for the Reformation of Manners, 90–91
virtue and, 11

Wollaston, William, 21

Libertarianism.org

Liberty. It's a simple idea and the linchpin of a complex system of values and practices: justice, prosperity, responsibility, toleration, cooperation, and peace. Many people believe that liberty is the core political value of modern civilization itself, the one that gives substance and form to all the other values of social life. They're called libertarians.

Libertarianism.org is the Cato Institute's treasury of resources about the theory and history of liberty. The book you're holding is a small part of what Libertarianism.org has to offer. In addition to hosting classic texts by historical libertarian figures and original articles from modern-day thinkers, Libertarianism.org publishes podcasts, videos, online introductory courses, and books on a variety of topics within the libertarian tradition.

Cato Institute

Founded in 1977, the Cato Institute is a public policy research foundation dedicated to broadening the parameters of policy debate to allow consideration of more options that are consistent with the principles of limited government, individual liberty, and peace. To that end, the Institute strives to achieve greater involvement of the intelligent, concerned lay public in questions of policy and the proper role of government.

The Institute is named for Cato's Letters, libertarian pamphlets that were widely read in the American Colonies in the early 18th century and played a major role in laying the philosophical foundation for the American Revolution.

Despite the achievement of the nation's Founders, today virtually no aspect of life is free from government encroachment. A pervasive intolerance for individual rights is shown by government's arbitrary intrusions into private economic transactions and its disregard for civil liberties. And while freedom around the globe has notably increased in the past several decades, many countries have moved in the opposite direction, and most governments still do not respect or safeguard the wide range of civil and economic liberties.

To address those issues, the Cato Institute undertakes an extensive publications program on the complete spectrum of policy issues. Books, monographs, and shorter studies are commissioned to examine the federal budget, Social Security, regulation, military spending, international trade, and myriad other issues. Major policy conferences are held throughout the year, from which papers are published thrice yearly in the *Cato Journal*. The Institute also publishes the quarterly magazine *Regulation*.

In order to maintain its independence, the Cato Institute accepts no government funding. Contributions are received from foundations, corporations, and individuals, and other revenue is generated from the sale of publications. The Institute is a nonprofit, tax-exempt, educational foundation under Section 501(c)3 of the Internal Revenue Code.

CATO INSTITUTE
1000 Massachusetts Ave., N.W.
Washington, D.C. 20001
www.cato.org